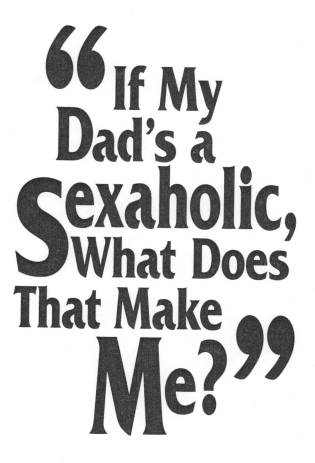

"If My Dad's a Sexaholic, What Does That Make Me?"

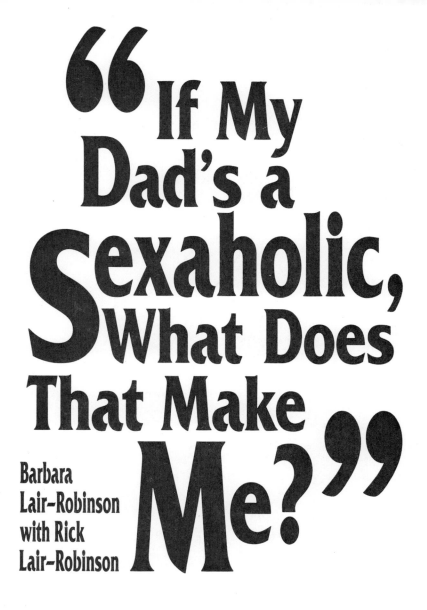

"If My Dad's a Dad's a Sexaholic, What Does That Make Me?"

Barbara
Lair-Robinson
with Rick
Lair-Robinson

CompCare® Publishers

Minneapolis, Minnesota

Lair Robinson, Barbara, 1951-
        If My Dad's A Sexaholic, What Does That Make Me?/Barbara Lair
Robinson with Rick Lair Robinson.
        p. cm.
        Includes bibliographical references.
        ISBN 0-89638-234-6
1. Adult children of sex addicts—Mental health. 2. Adult children of sex
addicts—Family relationships. I. Lair Robinson, Rick. II. Title.
RC569.5.A32L35 1991   90-20602
616.85'83—dc20   CIP

Cover and interior design by MacLean and Tuminelly.

Inquiries, orders, and catalog requests should be addressed to:
CompCare Publishers
2415 Annapolis Lane
Minneapolis, MN 55441
Call toll free 800/328-3330
(Minnesota residents 612/559-4800)

5	4	3	2	1
95	94	93	92	91

We dedicate this book to our families – the families we grew up with. We have found more love, stability, and fun than we ever dreamed possible.

Our thanks to friends and families from Fountain Centers in Albert Lea, Minnesota, St. Mary's Hospital in Minneapolis, Presbyterian Hospital and Freedom of Choice in Oklahoma City, and Gateways in Roseburg, Oregon.

Our gratitude to the Eagles Nest Restaurant and to our friends in Oklahoma for their support during the most difficult time in our lives.

Finally we send our love to Dick Selvig, who knew so many years ago what the rest of us keep discovering

In memory of Don Anderson and Tiger. Everyone needs a best friend and a good dog. They were God's brief blessing to us.

Barbara and Rick Lair Robinson

Contents

Introduction

"If my dad's a sexaholic, what does that make me?" I remember running that thought through my mind the first time I heard my father introduce himself in a recovery group as "a sexaholic." That day in 1983, my dad had found his core addiction and relief from the symptoms that had plagued him for as long as I can remember. Since then, I've been discovering a different understanding of myself and my family than I had before I shifted my attention from the dynamics of chemical dependency in families to those of sex addiction.

My family has been greatly blessed by my parents' search for spiritual healing. Several family crises during the mid-1960s in Minneapolis led my parents to be among the first who sought support and a framework for living in a self-help program that focused on emotional health. In 1967 we moved to Montana, where a group of recovering alcoholics took in my dad and mom because my parents' group was not available there. Oddly enough, three recovering alcoholics in Bozeman had been members of AA during its early days in New York. The wisdom and love of this group inspired my father, and one incredible woman became my mother's best friend. Even with all this attention from people who understood addiction, it would still be ten years before my mother discovered her drug addiction, and sixteen years before my father's understanding of sex addiction changed his life.

I don't think *denial* of problems held my parents back so much as the *seeming normalcy* of those problems. Alcoholism has troubled generations of my mother's family, and alcoholism and sex addiction were equally familiar problems in my father's family. My mother's upbringing in a strict, fundamental Catholic home taught her to adapt, no matter what the circumstances. My father's early life had been so much worse than his adulthood that he felt he was on his way up.

My parents went through many exciting times and many terrible times during the ten years following the move to Montana. Finally, when Mom fell apart in the right place at the right time, she discovered that she was addicted to prescription "medication" and alcohol, and began treatment for chemical dependency. During the next three years, she intervened in her children's addiction; of five siblings, four of us are alcoholics and drug addicts. After many treatments and family weeks, Dad added yet another recovery program, this time one for family members of alcoholics. I remember his excitement in family weeks. "We've discovered the problem," he said. "Everybody is alcoholic!" One courageous treatment center in Minnesota even organized a special week of inpatient therapy for my parents' marriage.

Still, Dad's symptoms didn't go away. He was increasingly out of touch with his impact on others, more intimidating to talk with — much less confront — and more hooked on power, money, and material things. Mom had discovered that Dad was having affairs, and their marriage threatened to break. All we could do was wish that he drank so we could get him into treatment for *something*. Unfortunately, knowledge about sex addiction was a few years away.

Finally, in 1983, my mother heard about a new recovery program for people with sex addiction. She confronted my father about his sexaholism when he began setting up an old pattern that could have led to another affair. Although he'd stopped having affairs a few years before, he was like an alcoholic who quits drinking but doesn't find a different way to live. As Dad began attending a self-help program for sexaholics, he immediately knew he was home.

Dad didn't dream that his thinking and therefore his interactions were sexualized, probably from childhood. He thought he lived in the same world as everyone else. As he puts it, "I didn't know what sexaholism was, just like a fish doesn't know what water is, because it's all that the fish has ever known." He further explained with an example. Whenever he saw a man drive up to a house at noontime, Dad assumed he was going over to his mistress's house for sex. It never occurred to Dad that most of the world thinks the man is going home for lunch.

Mom was the perfect co-addict. She laughs at the memory of living in an apartment complex that was apparently notorious as a place where rich, older executives "kept" their young women. Mom simply thought it was nice that all those fathers spent time with their daughters. In the years of Dad's recovery, Mom has talked about the pain of examining her co–sex addiction. She remembers the boring routine and stability in her upbringing, the excitement of Dad's romancing, and her fear a few weeks into their marriage that something was terribly wrong. But she did what she knew how to do: she adapted.

My father is a teacher. Our conversations during the past seven years of his recovery have taught me to understand and recognize important characteristics of sex addiction. When I submitted a paper to a conference of the National Association on Sex Addiction Problems, I entitled it, "If My Dad's a Sexaholic, What Does That Make Me?" The conference accepted my paper, but they changed the title to "Adult Children of Sex Addicts." I tackled this title by talking about characteristics of sexaholism that I had observed in my personal experience and my work as a family counselor. I described the impact of these characteristics on the addict's and co-addict's life; how they affect the family as an environment; and what the children learn and carry into adulthood. The more information my husband (who is also a counselor) and I found, the more I realized that this title provided me personally a new feeling of belonging.

I have listened to many men and women who, like myself, reinterpreted our experiences according to the program of Adult Children of Alcoholics, or who generalized our experiences to fit the program of Adult Children of Dysfunctional Families. I would think, "Well, I remember having similar feelings. I never really had an experience like that, but . . ." I always believed that the emotions and consequences for individuals from "dysfunctional families" were more similar than different, so we could all find what we needed in ACOA or ACODF. These groups blaze the trail, but now I see that the people with whom I really identify are those who, like me, were children of either sexaholics or sexually dysfunctional families. A woman at one of my lectures pointed out that, unless you have the right focus, you can't do the necessary First Step work in a recovery program. (See the reprinted Twelve Steps on pages 178–179.) As the saying goes, "How can you know where you're going if you don't know where you came from?"

My father needed to know that he was a sexaholic in order to learn, grow, and survive. He continues to grow, with the help of his recovery program and people who share his problem. I have shared information with enough adult children to recognize that we also need the unqualified spark of recognition that comes with this shared family experience.

Even though my own primary recovery is from drugs and alcohol, I, like my father, needed to fill the empty loneliness that I did not even know existed. I will never forget hearing my father speak to a group about recovery from sex addiction and breaking down, saying, "I finally found birds with feathers like mine." His long search, assisted by many wonderful people in self-help programs, was finally over. He was home. And I began a new journey.

Chapter One

Adult Children of Sex Addicts

hy do we need another focus and recovery program? The answer is simple: to offer solutions, support, and understanding for a different set of problems. A child growing up in alcoholism walks through the door and finds a parent passed out on the floor in the entryway. Children growing up in sex addiction walk through the front door to a totally different experience. We may not bring our friends home because a parent is suggestive sexually, or even "hitting on" our friends. We may stumble across pornography, hear hushed stories about our parents, or even have to "accept" at an early age that a parent has affairs or a "love" relationship with someone other than our mom or dad.

Many children, particularly when they get older, find out that they have brothers or sisters they never knew about. Children may overhear phone calls, catch a parent in an affair, have to listen about a parent's emotional pain, or helplessly watch a parent go "crazy," and not have a clue that a sex addiction is the driving force. Many children, girls and boys, grow into adulthood demeaning themselves and each other by using sex as a means of getting and keeping relationships or to chalk up "notches on a bedpost" or to keep up a sad image. Many children are being used sexually by a parent, and walk through the door each day to this burden.

Some of the problems that come from our experiences growing up in sexually addicted or sexually dysfunctional families are common to all children from dysfunctional families. There is no question that many addictions overlap in their symptoms. However, each addiction also has a unique impact on our lives; the knowledge that one other human being has had similar experiences is the beginning of all recoveries.

My husband says he will always remember the first time he saw the First Step of Alcoholics Anonymous. He nearly jumped out of his chair screaming, "Of course! I CAN'T drink alcohol." This revelation was quickly followed by rage as he looked around the room thinking, why the hell didn't somebody just say so?

But as time passed, a new thought began to creep in, "If somebody wrote that line, they must understand exactly what's wrong. And if they know what's wrong, maybe they know what to do about it." When a person sees that others have recovered from problems, like his own, he can begin to find the freedom and courage to recover.

I am one of the lucky ones. Knowing that my father is an acknowledged sex addict, I see my experience verified. I don't think I could have pieced together enough information to realize that sex addiction was my father's problem. I had access to only bits and pieces of information about his sexual acting out. More to the point, who had ever heard of sex addiction? When my father told us that he had joined a group for recovering sexaholics, I went through all the predictable reactions. (Gosh, Dad, maybe you just need to work on your recovery a little harder.) Thanks to my father's openness and especially the recovery in his life, acceptance came quickly. The beauty of understanding his sex addiction was that Dad's behavior now made sense. And my own problems began to make sense as well.

Some areas of my life seemed impenetrable, despite the fact that I was armed with many years of recovery from drug and alcohol addiction. I kept battering away at these areas with my time-tested strategies to no avail, but I continued to do it anyway. It reminded me of Emily, our stubborn bulldog pup. She used to sit by the front door for hours on end, waiting for it to open so she could get out. She never did realize that there was a back door, and she only had to give it a push and walk out. What I see now is more than one way out.

In many lectures I have described the characteristic ways a sex addict deals with his world and relationships. Without fail, people come up to tell me, "That sounds like my (father, mother, husband, wife, boss, friend)." Many readers will piece together information in this book and identify strongly with adult children of sex addicts. Even if most of the pieces fit, however, families may not support or acknowledge that this understanding of the family history is true. A member of Adult Children of Sex Addicts (now Adult Children of Sexually Dysfunctional Families) recently told me, "Some people who identified strongly with the characteristics of adult children of sex addicts couldn't identify a compulsive pattern in a parent. For that reason, we expanded our materials to include sexually dysfunctional families as well as sex addiction."

As the field of sex addiction treatment grows, and it has to, children of sex addicts will have access to the answers and the support of others who preceded them to light their paths. We hope that those others will be us.

ADULT CHILDREN OF SEX ADDICTS: CHARACTERISTICS

What is it like to grow up as a child of a sex addict? We think it is important to see that we are not unique because of the sex addiction that has shaped our lives. The Twelve Step groups that preceded us have already learned the hard lessons of "terminal uniqueness." We are a people who feel lonely and alone, believing deep down that no one could possibly understand the pain we feel. But what is the sense of discovering our "problem" if we wind up continuing to feel "different"? Dick Selvig, a pioneer in the field of addiction, always said that we must first find out how we are similar to others, not how we are different. Learning that we share something with others is the first part in our spiritual healing.

We state characteristics reluctantly because they have so much potential for overgeneralization, oversimplification, and every other "ation" there is. We don't claim to be uniquely affected by these characteristics. At the same time, many people who search for a home, a place filled with people like themselves, need help to understand what makes them similar. While some traits are common to many dysfunctions, sex addiction often leaves its own mark. Many people who relate to the following characteristics may not know that they grew up in a family afflicted with sex addiction. It would be rare, however, that an adult child of a sex addict or sexually dysfunctional family would not relate to the characteristics described below.

1. Many of us experience such confusion or fear and shame about our sexuality that our relationships are affected.
2. Many of us have given sex expecting love in return, only to lose the person we wanted to love us and to feel ashamed and confused.
3. Many of us gain weight, dress unattractively, or find other ways to isolate and insulate ourselves from intimacy and sexual relationships.

4. Many of us diet and exercise compulsively and are obsessive about our appearance.

5. Many of us will find ourselves lying, storytelling, telling half-truths, or misrepresenting ourselves, even when we intend not to, in order to impress someone, stay out of trouble, or get something we want. We feel that who we really are, without embellishment, isn't good enough.

6. Many of us are withdrawn, or we go through the motions of life in deep depression.

7. Many of us are constantly drawn to chaos by inner agitation and restlessness.

8. Many of us travel from one compulsive outlet to the next, wondering what is wrong with us and why we cannot stop.

9. Many of us stay in relationships with people who say they love us, but who sexually abuse or degrade us, either physically or verbally.

10. Many of us have thought that suspicion, jealousy, and possessiveness are normal and even flattering elements of our relationships.

11. Many of us find ourselves in frightening or potentially dangerous sexual situations because of our inability to judge people and to say no.

12. Many of us have been seduced into abusive or degrading sexual situations in the name of "proving our love" or for fear of losing a relationship.

13. Others of us are abusive or resort to degradation and humiliation in our close relationships. The closer people get, the more abusive we become.

14. Often, the anxiety that comes with asserting ourselves, saying no, or attempting to leave a relationship causes us to doubt ourselves, to think we are crazy or selfish. That anxiety may drive us back to unhealthy situations.

15. Many of us have suffered great sexual and emotional trauma from childhood, many at the hands of our family or friends of our family.

16. Many of us have felt trapped in relationships with mates who were unfaithful and otherwise abusive.

17. Most of us suffer from being either too close or too
distant in relationships; we cannot find a healthy balance.
18. Many of us would do and have done anything to perpetuate a relationship because we were afraid to be alone.
19. Many of us desperately want recovery, but, confronted
with the unhealthy habits in our lives, we vigorously and
automatically defend everything we want so badly to give up.
This defense is born of a uniquely pervasive shame and the
need for control that characterizes sex addiction's impact on
families.

CHILDREN OF SEX ADDICTS: THE EXPERIENCE

A child growing up in alcoholism understands emptying
bottles, seeing Dad drunk at the class play, and hearing "crazy
talk" when he's been drinking. He also understands hiding
bottles and not bringing friends home because Mom may
already be half in the bag. He understands the terms "mean
drunk," "sloppy drunk," "quiet drunk," and "I like him better
drunk than sober."

   We would like to present some composite experiences of
adult children of sexaholics. Our hope is that adult children
might begin to see and hear their own story from others and
realize that they are not alone, that other people have had
their experience. It is a great relief for us as adults to know
that someone else saw things pretty much as we did.

ANN

Ann was the shoulder her mom cried on about her father's
affairs. She felt increasingly sorry for her mother and angry
at her father. To add to her confusion, these incidents usually
ended with her parents making up and acting more in love
than ever. She finally got so angry at her father that she
encouraged her mother to leave him. After a particularly
long-term affair, Ann's mother finally seemed to be ready to
take some action, but at the last moment returned to her

husband once again. Ann felt betrayed, alienated, and guilty, but she didn't dare leave her role as confidante. She felt her mother needed her; in fact, she needed to be needed by her mother.

Ann didn't understand or necessarily see the sexual dysfunction in her family, but she demonstrated it throughout her life. Her brothers showed no respect for women and commonly talked about women and sex abusively in her presence. She herself was sexually promiscuous as an adolescent, thinking sex was her only bargaining chip in the all-important drive to "get a man." Ann married twice. Her first husband was a man she married after knowing him for only three weeks; he had affairs and fathered children outside their marriage. She didn't love her second husband, who was insanely jealous and possessive. Although she lived alone for brief periods, she felt terrified and worthless without a man. Her anxiety led to many one-night stands and a few unhealthy relationships, all very sexually oriented. Ann had three children along the way, and, because she didn't know how to take care of herself, much less her children, they were severely affected.

The most difficult recovery issue Ann faces is her fear and shame about herself as a sexual being. She eats compulsively and works compulsively, as she faces recovery in this area of her life. The family she grew up in is burdened to various degrees with all these compulsive outlets. Ann is also painfully aware of these issues in her children's lives and is trying to help them as she is being helped.

CARRIE

When she was fourteen years old, Carrie found her mother in bed with a strange man. She learned eventually that her mother had been having affairs for years and would not stop, despite her promises. They set up an unspoken system of blackmail whereby the mother allowed Carrie to party with her friends; in exchange Carrie kept her mother's affairs secret from her dad. She came to our attention when she entered treatment for alcoholism and drug addiction. She had made little progress, and we received little cooperation from Carrie's parents.

Once we began meeting with the whole family and watched them interact, it was obvious that Carrie had some unusual control over her mother. As our work progressed, the secrets came out and the family eventually entered intensive long-term therapy. Carrie's mother acknowledged her sex addiction and went to treatment.

Carrie's story about her relationships and her sexuality is very similar to Ann's. Most significant to Carrie was her mistaken belief that sex meant love and her lack of awareness that her relationships were severely limited because her interactions were so sexualized. She finally realized her fears about her sexuality after marriage and children slowed down her sex life with her husband. She worried that her marriage was falling apart.

She also put herself in scary predicaments with men she met at work because she didn't know how to refuse their frequent sexual advances. Carrie was ashamed that she was doing something wrong to attract these guys. All she knew was to say things like, "I can't go out with you—I'm married." Or, "I'll have lunch with you, but only as a friend. Okay?" She was so fearful of offending a man that she made her excuses and then quickly said something flattering and "flirty" to avoid hurting their feelings. She began gaining weight, and when she was fifty pounds overweight, the attention stopped.

Carrie looks back now with sadness about her limited skills for making her way in the world. She regrets that her anger caused her to refuse when her mother offered her money for a therapist who understood the family dynamics of sex addiction. She is also angry at the superficial way her treatment center dealt with the sexual issues in her life. She kept hearing, "Just stay off drugs and alcohol and out of relationships for a year, and everything will work itself out." Carrie finally went into therapy and is in recovery from alcoholism, overeating, and spending money. She is now working through problems that stem from her childhood with a sex-addicted mom and an alcoholic father.

JOHN

John remembers spending as much time at the home of his father's mistress as he did in his own home. Of four children, he was the only one his father took with him on those visits, and he liked that special attention. John loved going over to the house and playing with the woman's children, but knew he had to keep the visit secret for some reason. He remembers his overwhelming thoughts and feelings when he finally was old enough to figure out what was going on between his father and this woman, and what that meant for his mother. To make matters more difficult, he found out that the children he had played with all those years were his father's. John focused all his pain and anger on the other woman, whom he had loved, and at his mother, because she had been unable to keep her husband. John was sexually promiscuous as an adult and lost a few relationships with women he loved. His wife had affairs and eventually left him for another man. John lost another woman he loved because he was too scared to make a commitment.

MARY LEE

Mary Lee had grown up with rules that didn't always feel right. Her father was the only one who had the right to walk into bedrooms when the doors were closed; he sometimes "accidently" walked in while she was dressing. Her father made her come into the bathroom while he was taking a shower so he could talk to her. When he made her sit on his lap, his hands often roamed, and if she squirmed uncomfortably, he told her he was trying to be loving and affectionate. He started having sex with her before she was nine years old. As she grew older, her father became more demanding, blatant, and perverse in the demands he made on her. Mary Lee just shook her head in bewilderment when asked by her group, "Where was your mother?"

Now that she was married, Mary Lee's father hounded her. When she refused to see him, he wrote her "love letters" referring to their "special love (sex) relationship" and spelling out his use of her in his fantasy life. Mary Lee was involved in three years of intensely painful therapy about this abuse. She says her one piece of gratitude, ironically, is that her memories were not blocked or repressed like those of so many incest survivors. She thought it would have been unbearably painful to have so many problems with sex and relationships without knowing why, and the recognition of memories from the recesses of her mind would have terrified her. Mary Lee thought often about suicide before and during her therapy.

KATHY

Kathy was embarrassed to bring friends home because her mother wanted to hang around and flirt with her boyfriends. Kathy sometimes accused her mother of coming on to the guys, but her mom always ended these confrontations making Kathy feel crazy and ashamed of herself. Kathy had heard her parents fighting about sex, her father begging her mother to "love" him. Kathy felt ashamed of the contempt she felt toward her father for putting up with her mother's abuse. She withdrew more and more from her own sexuality and became more and more asexual in appearance. She became obsessed with exercise and with her weight, starving herself to the point of being hospitalized.

JAMES

Although his father was a minister in a strict, fundamentalist church, James vaguely remembers seeing pictures of his parents with some people he didn't know, and all of them were nude. He believes he once saw his dad with a strange woman in his parents' bed, but when he talked to his mother about it, she told him he was imagining it. James knows his dad was asked to leave one ministry when he was accused of drinking and having an affair with the church secretary, but no one except his sister will talk with him about it. Now that all of the children are adults, they have split into factions over the issue of their father's drinking and sexual behavior. James has often wondered whether he's crazy and just made up the whole story. All the kids in this family experience serious problems about their sexuality and their religious beliefs. Two have had affairs during their marriages; one sister refuses sex with her husband for months at a time; and one brother is alienated from the family for being gay. Some of the kids are also chemically dependent.

JAN

The best relationship Jan ever had was with her big, strong, handsome father. She was his princess. He traded presents for sex and always gave her special treatment. Jan hated the sex but loved her father and the attention she got from him. She also hated it that her dad frequently beat up her three brothers and that her mother didn't stop him. Jan has gone through many painful relationships and has been sexually abused as a grown woman by male and female sexual partners. She is in therapy for chemical dependency and incest. Now that she is taking antidepressants, she has stopped trying to kill herself.

The most painful consequence for Jan as an adult is her inability to have nurturing relationships with friends. She either gets too close and is rejected, or stays too distant, trying not to get too close. She feels safer and more comfortable in loving relationships with women. She is trying to come to terms with her mother now that she and her father are divorced. She is working with her therapist on the best way to intervene with her brother, who she believes is sexually abusing children.

After reading these sketches, you may be remembering incidents from your own past. Maybe you can understand the predicament of children trying to develop as thinking, feeling, sexual, and spiritual beings in families traumatized by generations of increasingly oppressive dysfunction.

The best image to illustrate family function is a huge, old tree that has been around for generations. This tree is in a thriving forest, and all the conditions were right for it to grow straight and strong and tall. If you look at its root system, you find an enormous, intricate maze of roots holding the tree firmly in its place and supplying the nourishment it needs to thrive.

Now imagine a tree, intended to grow straight and strong, forced to grow out the side of a cliff as the edge has given way. The tree doesn't know its predicament. It simply changes the direction of its root structure in order to stabilize itself and thus survive. Amazingly, many of these trees not only survive but eventually thrive.

When alcoholism and sex addiction began shaping my family's heritage some generations ago, the people didn't know what they were dealing with; they just did the best they could with what they had and sent their roots in the direction necessary for survival. My family, like many others, also were forced to cope against incredible odds over and above the addictions that held us captive. We were presented with one backbreaking trauma after the other, mostly in the form of illness and forced change. When I heard Robert Ackerman say that the term *dysfunction* means "functioning in pain," and not "wrong," "bad," or "sick," I knew that was an accurate description of my family's behavior. We functioned in pain, all the while searching for the answers and solutions that would help us to the health we're finding today.

Working for several years to facilitate multi-family therapy groups, I've listened to countless men and women over sixty years old, who have remembered alcoholic parents and grandparents dating back to life in the late 1800s. The enabling, the abuse, the refusal to face the reality of what was going on, the secrets, the shame, the kids leaving home to get away, and the cost to future generations are all there in the stories they told.

Now we use the term *denial*, when what may be going on isn't denial so much as normalcy. Five generations ago, when our family had its first alcoholic, when the first child flew into a rage about Father being a "no-good" drunk, he was slapped across the face and told, "Don't you ever say anything like that again. He's your father, and you respect him!" Maybe we can call this denial, but back then it was critical to go on, because the drunk father was the only person who could put food on the family's table. There was no welfare system to fall back on. In this family, four generations later, the practice of keeping secrets, compensating, and not rocking the boat was so ingrained in our interactions it never occurred to us before treatment that there is any different way.

Looking at memories of our troubled childhood is like looking at the rain, wind, and erosion that so obviously affected our tree's efforts to thrive. The obvious things we can see, remember, and talk about, however, are a world apart from what affected us most profoundly—the things we blocked out and can't discuss. We are not conscious of the direction of our "roots," forced by the day-to-day demands of addiction in our family.

As adult children of sex addicts we need to examine how we were affected by life in a family whose interactions were sexualized. We need to understand what happened to our emotional development as a result of living around such intense stimulation and chaos. What have we learned about relationships in an atmosphere of victims and victimizers? How limited is our understanding of intimacy and skills for relationships when our parent's primary sexual addiction established sexual dysfunction, sexual stereotyping, and sexual acting out in the family that taught us who we are as men and women?

The "root structure" our family life influenced has the power to kill our striving for health because it has developed outside our conscious awareness. Our way of relating to the world probably perpetuates the problems we want so badly to leave behind. We cannot approach our world in a different way and produce a different result. If you unearth our tree you will see the power of our illness in the misshapen root structure that developed to ensure our survival.

One typical problem in the lives of Adult Children of Sex Addicts, particularly those who abuse alcohol and drugs, is promiscuous sex. The guilt and shame of promiscuity is one of the most painful reasons many women have for seeking sobriety. Many of these women leave treatment centers feeling like new people, only to find themselves involved in the same shame-producing sexual encounters months later, this time with marginally healthy men in AA clubhouses. They came seeking the fresh air and healing light of a Twelve Step program, so why do they find themselves in the middle of a disastrous affair?

Because more than just a drug and alcohol problem are entangled deeply in their roots, and more help is needed. We simply do not know how to live another way. People tell us, "Make friends with him first," which we interpret to mean, go out on three dates and do something wholesome like bowling before we have sex the first time. And, for most, this is progress. But it is far from where we need to be.

As adult children of sex addicts, we need to study the dynamics that shaped who we are and how we deal with the world and our relationships. Once we understand how we meet our needs, giving up the behavior is a process of surrender in the spirit of the first three Steps (see pages 178–179). We cannot stop what we do not understand.

Many adult children of sex addicts now in treatment for other addictions like alcoholism are also being treated as sex addicts, if their sexual behavior is considered at all. Too many others are told simply not to "have a relationship for one year" and assured that their sexual issues will clear up in sobriety. Just as it isn't accurate to label as alcoholic the children of alcoholics, the children of sex addicts are not necessarily addicts themselves. Many children of alcoholics abuse alcohol, but it isn't accurate to label them alcoholic on the basis of that fact alone. Some have crossed the line into addiction, but many are simply suffering from familial alcoholism or sex addiction, or the effects of their family dysfunctions, and their abuse will stop with therapy and Twelve Step work.

Adult children of sex addicts need a niche of their own. Not everyone who experiences a characteristic of an addiction is an addict. Professional help should always be considered to aid us in our search for answers. More therapists are learning to address this newly recognized disorder. They will provide the best diagnostic help and direction for the children developing in homes where sex addiction has been a driving force.

Chapter Two

Sex Addiction and Families

Many people assume that all sex addicts are greasy old derelicts like the man in the song, "Aqualung." Therapists practicing in this new addiction field are still trying to develop helpful images of the individuals needing treatment. Years ago, therapists who treated alcoholics faced a similar challenge when they confronted the stereotype of the skid row bum. The truth turned out to be quite different. Study and research revealed that only 3 percent of our nation's alcoholics could be found on "skid row." Who were the rest? Why, people like thee and me. Surprise!

So who are our sex addicts and what images of them come to mind? Like other groups of people, sex addicts vary greatly. At one extreme, they are incredibly dynamic, charismatic individuals who draw people to them. The media have been filled with stories of nationally known individuals at the height of their careers who self-destructed because of their sexual behavior. As my father learned, an untreated sex addict's penchant for power may result in great success, which eventually ends in sorrow and pain.

At the other extreme are people we tend to avoid. They are pathetic and unattractive, the people who give us "creepy" feelings. Society has a collective image of the dirty pervert stalking grade school playgrounds and heavy breathers wearing rubber raincoats. The great tragedy of these extremes is that they are the outlying trees and a whole forest lies between.

It is our task to teach the public who sex addicts really are. Although the work is incomplete, much has been done to bring the picture into focus, particularly by individuals such as Patrick Carnes, author of *Out of the Shadows* and *Contrary to Love*, and groups such as Sexaholics Anonymous and Sex Addicts Anonymous. And if we look closely at this developing picture we will see people just like ourselves, with families just like our own.

Our desire is to do more than help clarify the picture of the sex addict and ease the stigma that currently exists. We also wish to develop a deeper understanding of the illness, and in order to do this, we must look at the whole picture. The sex addict is not the illness; he is just one individual affected by the disease. This book is concerned with the effects of the illness on the whole family, particularly the children of sex addicts.

SEX ADDICTS DO HAVE FAMILIES

Dr. Carl Whitaker, a teacher of family therapy, said in a workshop that marriage was simply ". . . two families sending out scapegoats to do battle and see whose family would be reproduced." Much of our behavior in a marriage comes from our original families. If we grew up in a family burdened with addiction and compulsions, we take that experience and its lessons with us when we look for a mate and a new family. We typically see our role in relationships dimly and are aware of only a fraction of the forces that shape our lives.

I read a sad example of this fact in an article by Patrick Carnes, "The Spiraling Cycle of Compulsion and Denial," which told a story about a sexually addicted woman named Ruth. She is a recovering alcoholic woman whose "sexuality problem" did not take care of itself in recovery as the chemical dependency treatment staff promised it would. Instead her life was consumed by her sex addiction—the shame, the pain, the sexual acting out, the attempts to control her behavior, and the consequences. "The despair component of her addictive cycle was vicious," Carnes writes. "The worst moments were the weekends her son was gone and she had unstructured days. Drugs helped her cope since she could spend the days in oblivion until her son returned."

This story is Ruth's and not her son's, but I imagine the special predicament of this child, growing up unaware in the tangle of his mother's sex addiction. As an adult, he will certainly identify with many of the characteristics of adult children of sex addicts, but what if he believes that no sex addiction existed in his family? In alcoholism intervention, families are usually called upon to inform the alcoholic of the amount and frequency of her drinking and the seriousness of its effects. While denial and delusion still abound, the presence of the bottle at least provides physical proof to which her children can connect memories. And because we understand the label "alcoholism," we can help families understand why they feel so crazy and what they can do about it. Because sex addiction is masked by other issues, Ruth's son probably would not put the pieces together without her cooperation and professional help.

Except in cases of incest, most parents' sex addiction plays out behind their children's backs. At a conscious level, kids may have access only to the tip of the iceberg. They may find a stack of pornography, which the parent explains away.

Worse yet, he or she may not explain it at all, and the child is left to reconcile the incongruent teachings and behavior. Children might overhear arguments that scare them. As therapists, we commonly treat children who hear their parents arguing behind closed doors and wonder what bad thing they did to make their parents so upset. A child may even catch a parent in an affair, but even then, few children of sex addicts can put the pieces together. As more sex addicts step forward for help, we will be looking at their children to see how they fare and whether parents pass on sex addiction from one generation to the next.

Children who grow up in alcoholic homes are rarely able to use alcohol appropriately. ACOAs have learned a great deal about drinking from the important people around them, which includes not just parents, but other relatives, friends, film personalities, athletes, and whomever else they take as role models. Not surprisingly, ACOAs tend either to abuse alcohol or abstain with scorn, looking down on those who do drink.

An ACOA who cannot make contact with others because of intense shyness and low self-worth might discover the "magic" of alcohol one night by having a few drinks and feeling like the life of the party. This experience may not make her alcoholic, but it certainly shows what she has learned about the use of alcohol.

Adult children of sex addicts rarely have fulfilling sex lives or healthy attitudes about sexuality in general. Sex tends to be humiliating, abusive, forced, frightening, addictive, or absent. An ACOSA may feel intensely vulnerable in a dating situation and know how to make contact or regain his bearings only by means of sex or the manipulations typically associated with unhealthy sex. This behavior may not make him a sex addict, but it shows that he is vulnerable to using sex in an unhealthy but familiar way. These adult children do not usually have any idea that they view the world and relationships through filters which are colored by the family dynamics of sex addiction.

Jennie and Mike, a mother and her twenty-two-year-old son who are both in recovery from alcoholism, demonstrate these dynamics. Jennie grew up with two parents who were sex addicts, and Mike's father was a sex addict. (Their complete story can be found on page 155.) Most of Mike's recovery problems revolve around the issue of his sexuality and relationships. He tends to pick "bad girls" who want sex immediately, and when he approaches them, he freezes and can't or won't follow through. He considers himself a male version of a "tease." When he was eight or ten years old, this same young man was playing a game with the little neighborhood kids that resembled hide-and-seek, but the kids called it "rape." Mike's younger brother, Tim, is just the opposite: He just lost another nice girlfriend because he was so "rude." Tim attracts "prudes" and then offends them by pushing them sexually and by being rude and vulgar. Fortunately for these two boys, their mother is putting the pieces of her background together and coming up with sex addiction in the family she grew up in. Information about the way sex addiction affects the family will be crucial to their recovery.

LOOKING THROUGH A GLASS DARKLY

You would think that anyone would know whether he grew up in sex addiction, but many people we've talked with cannot see what is clear to others. John was preparing to attend a post-traumatic stress workshop for Vietnam Vets. He remembered his mother shaking her breasts in his face from the time he was little and asking him, "Look at these titties, aren't these the greatest titties you ever saw?" His father came home in rages and asked "How was your mother in bed? I know you probably slept with her; how was she?" His sister and her girlfriends danced provocatively around his room, and if he moved to leave, they screamed RAPE, which provoked a beating from his father. When he was a grown man, his sister came to see him once when he was in jail and asked, "So, do you want to have sex with me?"

These incidents pale when woven into his entire story, and it is no wonder John was experiencing a period of impotence. I am very careful about using the term *incest*, but this seemed as appropriate a place for the word as any. I told him that survivors of incest and sexual abuse experience post-traumatic stress syndrome like the one that necessitated his hospitalization after Vietnam. I encouraged him to use the upcoming workshop to discuss family issues as well as his Vietnam experience.

He said to me, "But there wasn't any incest or sexual abuse in my family." As my father observed, a child of sex addicts doesn't recognize the dysfunction in his family, just like a fish doesn't know what water is because it's all the fish has ever known.

Many sex addicts do not sexually abuse their children, who may not know what is going on outside the home with mom and dad. Many ACOSAs therefore leave home not identifying sexual addiction as a problem. Many incest survivors block out the experience for years. Even when they remember, they may resist the idea that the incest perpetrator is a sex addict. A friend of mine said, "Don't you let my father off the hook by telling him him he has a disease!" As the sex-addiction model and the Twelve Steps help more perpetrators, perhaps we will be able to break down the stigma which now prevents people from talking and getting help. Adult children of sex addicts must learn that this addiction exists before they can recognize it. Only then can they piece together scattered bits of information about their family experience and understand how some of their living problems logically stem from childhood.

In my own case, I found out in my mid-twenties that my dad was having affairs. I certainly did not put together this knowledge with the "alcoholic personality" characteristics and think, "AHA! Dad's a sex addict!" I simply adapted to this new "plot twist" with the intensity characteristic of this family problem and tried to save my mother by being her confidante.

Sex addiction is emerging as a significant problem in our society, and sex addicts do have spouses and children. Huge numbers of such children need treatment. As it stands now, most people receiving help from addiction-oriented therapy and Twelve Step groups do not know yet that there is such a program as Adult Children of Sex Addicts. They glean what they can from other programs. Even when people hear the term, they may not apply it to themselves. Once when I was preparing for a lecture about children of sex addicts, a woman in the audience gasped and said, "Oh my God, I just realized *I'm* an adult child of a sex addict." If we begin to attract members of the other Twelve Step groups who can gain further insight into their lives, then the addition of yet another program is worthwhile. Welcome to another journey!

I'LL NEVER PUT MY KIDS THROUGH WHAT I WENT THROUGH

I've often heard adult children of sex addicts say, "I knew life was crazy and now I understand why. But don't you worry, I'll never put my kids through what I went through!"

It was fascinating to hear Mark Schwartz, Sc.D., clinical director of the Sexual Trauma Program at River Oaks Hospital, New Orleans, Louisiana, discuss the work being done with victims and perpetrators of sexual abuse. I was touched as he talked about the fine line between victims and victimizers. In our work with families, most of the sex addicts we've known who were sexually abused as children became abusers. Only a few did not.

Despite their efforts to make a different life for themselves and their children, these painful issues come up later in their lives. It's sad and frightening for these adult children to learn how typical it is for a person raised in a dysfunctional family to be attracted to someone from the same dysfunction. An incest survivor often marries an incest perpetrator, and a child of an alcoholic often marries an alcoholic or another child of an alcoholic. The very experience they are trying to escape finds its way into the marriage which some hoped would be their salvation, and which others sought as the lesser of two evils, a way to escape from home.

It is vital for adult children to recognize how common it is to grow up being physically, sexually, and verbally abused and then to find themselves, one horrible day, abusing their own children. Or to grow up hating a mother or father for having affairs and yet to find themselves, a few years into their marriage, in bed with a stranger for a one-night stand on a business trip.

My own life exemplifies the adaptation that results in the attraction to partners and friends with similar histories. I thought that a man's passivity was kindness and gentleness, proof that I wouldn't get hurt. What I didn't know was that passivity also meant that he couldn't hold a job, wasn't interested in anything, and could easily be "led" into affairs with any woman who wanted him. The passivity I looked for was a reaction to the family I grew up in.

I watched others look for "exciting" mates. They were exciting all right, and the flip side of all that excitement was abuse and cruelty. This self-destruction has another reaction to the families they grew up in. Some adult children took their high tolerance for excitement, agitation, and chaos and looked for the same level of tension in their relationships, while my response was to look for the opposite of excitement in a mate. Little did I know that I was the "exciting" one. I found myself agitating the chaos I knew, by raging, by being helpless, and by being horribly irresponsible in my relationships.

As we adult children grow up and our lives become more complex with the demands of relationships, parenting, career, money, and whatever else, our skills and ability to cope with these demands in a healthy way crumbles because they were at best only a fragile concept in our minds. We cannot do what we have not learned, and we cannot give what we never got. We may believe that, because we know about "healthy responses to stress," or have read a book about healthy communication with a spouse, or because we plan to do the "opposite" of what our parents did, that we are safe. A woman attending a family week with her son, who was in treatment, said, "I finally realized that 360 degrees from sick is sick!" She was determined to give her child a wonderful family experience, just the opposite of her pain-filled childhood.

Robert Ackerman said the term *dysfunction* means functioning in pain. This explanation of dysfunction strikes a chord most families are able to hear. If you ask a co-addict if she grew up in a dysfunctional family or a "sick" family she will probably say no. But tell her that the word *dysfunction* means "functioning in pain," and tears come to her eyes, and the story of her painful family experience follows. Most co-addicts I have worked with left one dysfunctional situation to marry into another . . . and another. Some co-addicts and children of sex addicts simply do not see the pain or the problems in their families because that is all they have ever known.

WHY WE NEED TO LOOK BACK

We often misuse words like "healthy" and "normal." What we see as "normal" may simply be whatever we're used to, not necessarily what the majority are doing. We sometimes assume that what goes on at home happens in everyone else's family as well. A forty-year-old woman told me a story that shows what I mean. Once when she had stayed overnight at another child's home, the father kissed them goodnight and left the room. Would he come back later, she asked her friend, for sex? She really thought that intercourse was ordinary behavior between fathers and daughters. Needless to say, she wasn't invited to spend the night again.

My husband remembers talking with the neighborhood kids after his cousin received one of his many beatings with a belt. They were all gathered around laughing and arguing about who had been hit the hardest and what their crimes had been. They never imagined that something might be wrong. Didn't everyone get hit with a belt?

When someone says nothing is wrong in his family, it's possible he's being quite honest, but he may not have a good handle on the truth. Despite the alcoholism and drug addiction evident in my family, if you had asked me then whether anything was wrong, I would have told you, "No, we have our problems but no more than anyone else." I truthfully didn't even see alcoholism, much less sex addiction. I was so caught up in the day-to-day problems, I couldn't see the larger picture.

Until circumstances force us to look at our lives in a new way, we may never question that our lives are anything but normal. Too often adult children of alcoholics come for help because they think they are "crazy" and only know they are falling apart. They come to the realization later that their parents were alcoholic. As we all learn, there is a lot of difference between honesty and truth. Truth, however different people experience it, implies a search of some sort, and this search may help us to see the many alternatives in our lives. Circumstances that encourage us to look back to the past, in our search for health in the present, are typically painful. Our marriage may be at stake. Perhaps our children are in trouble. Maybe anger and rage are surfacing that we didn't even know existed. We might be physically ill with life-threatening or chronic illnesses, or unable to escape a compulsion like eating, sex, spending, working . . . and it's doing damage to our lives. Maybe we can't stand another day of loneliness, maybe we can't hold a job or fulfill our potential, maybe we are falling apart physically. Perhaps we simply need to understand.

We realize that not everyone knows how to begin this search, so we have devised a way to get started.

There is a copy of the chart below on page 182. Readers who need more space may draw a layer on a piece of paper. The next few chapters will discuss the characteristics shown across the top of the chart and explore the impact of these characteristics on the addict's life, the co-addict's life, the family environment and the children's lives. As we go through each of these characteristics, readers may find it helpful to chart the dynamics and consequences that arouse emotions or feel familiar. The notes will probably make it easier to go back later and add more examples as the information stimulates thoughts and memories.

This material is so charged with feeling that readers may need to work awhile and take a break. The information may be new and painful even for people who are well into recovery.

	The Illusion of Normality	Mistaking Excitement for Intimacy	Control	Interactions Are Sexualized
Addict				
Co–addict				
Family as an Environment				
What the Children Learn and Take into Adulthood				

Chapter Three

The Illusion of Normality

Families who are struggling with a sex addiction may not see the addiction they are struggling with. This difficulty is the first and most important characteristic of sex addiction. Many people read books like this one and say that they would never have put up with such abuse in their own relationships. The reality is that they probably would have if they had been in someone else's shoes all their lives.

An even more interesting idea is that the same people who say they "would never live like that!" may, in fact, be living with a different version of the same story and not even be able to recognize it. Each person's problems are "normal" to her.

Jennie is a good example of adult children's blindness to their families' dysfunctions. She was the caretaker in a close relationship with an alcoholic, sex-addicted father who told her the details of his sex life until the day he died. Until she began recovery, however, she thought there was nothing unusual about his behavior. Such blindness is common. It is imperative to read this book with an open mind.

Becoming a person can be compared to building a home. When we lay the foundation, if we are given faulty materials, the day will come when our house will begin to crumble. If we go back to look at the faulty materials, they may look the same as the best on the surface.

Our personalities also develop from the foundation up. If our foundation is not laid "with the best materials," the day comes when we can no longer patch ourselves. When we get to this point, if we are lucky, we find help or help finds us. We must go back and examine our lives to understand, explore the consequences, heal, and change.

In my case, help found me when my parents intervened. I happened into recovery from alcoholism and drug addiction because my parents sent me to treatment and because, once I got there, people were nice to me. So I stayed. I didn't use any chemicals and I went to meetings and groups because that gave me entry into a new, fun social group, not because I recognized my addiction. I did all the therapy for me and my kids because that's what people did in Minnesota.

Because I stayed, time was on my side. I learned more about the problems at the very foundation of my life. What I learned caused me a great deal of pain and led to an enormous amount of work, but I still stayed.

After about two years of hard work my life had changed enough that I realized, very suddenly, that I really *was* an alcoholic and a drug addict. I could now see my addiction clearly. I had not consciously denied the truth about the life I had lived. Neither did my parents nor even their parents. We all did the best we could with what we were given and assumed that everyone else lived lives like our own. Our problems were "normal."

Houses and people built with faulty materials may stand for a long time before crumbling. Sadly, most people who begin to crumble can only try to solve their problems alone, or they get the wrong kind of help. Anyone who has found his way into recovery will tell you that his greatest wish for people struggling with addiction is that they "hit bottom." When that happens, the crumbling little house is swept away one day by a disaster. It takes a disaster in their lives that they can't fix for most people to find help and stay with it. *A disaster isn't necessary.* Any reader who is struggling can give up and reach out for help.

The addict's perception that her life is normal is much more than denial. The word *denial* suggests conscious awareness of a situation combined with the decision not to act on that awareness. What happens in addicted families is much more deeply ingrained and beyond our control than that. These families have an illusion of normalcy. Most of us are the third generation of dysfunction and addiction. Dysfunction is our norm.

This illusion develops through a prolonged and complex process. One piece of this process can be illustrated by talking about how responsibility is shared in relationships. In a healthy relationship, each partner "agrees" to share part of the overall load in the relationship. The load can be split up any number of ways. One partner, for example, might carry the financial load while the other carries the housekeeping and the bills. This same couple might share responsibilities with the children, and on the weekends everyone pitches in to get the work done so everyone can play. On an emotional level one partner might be better at talking, but the agreement isn't that the better talker speak for both. The agreement is that the better talker be patient, and the one who has a harder time keep working at saying what's on his mind. Agreements are made consciously or unconsciously about how we handle in-laws and extended family, what we do for fun, how we spend our money, how we argue, how and when we have sex, how we handle the kids, and on and on.

Sometimes, of course, circumstances force us to carry more than our share of the load, but these times are understood or planned for, and the hard times are talked through. A good example is the illness of one partner for a period of time. When one partner adds school to her load so the family can get ahead, or when a job puts special demands on a family, adjustments must be made. Everyone shifts the load to pick up some of the extra work. Family, friends, and church might help too. If the load continues too long without relief, however, even a healthy relationship becomes dysfunctional, with everyone losing touch with healthy skills and balance.

Families of addicts develop a different arrangement. Instead of a 50:50 relationship, the couple begins with a 75:25 division of labor at best. As the addiction worsens, the relationship becomes more unequal, until it might 95:5.

Adult children are in so much trouble because they grew up learning to carry too much or too little of a relationship. If I leave a family where I learned to carry 75 percent of the emotional and physical responsibilities in my relationships, whom do you think I need to find as a mate? My life, my way of coping with my world, makes it imperative that I take care of someone. And people who need to be taken care of have radar; their lives depend upon finding a caretaker. I can walk into a room where everything about me sends messages to people that I am capable in very special ways. Everyone may appreciate this about me, but the only people who *need* me as a caretaker are those who are unable to give their attention to a relationship. Sadly, if a co-addict or addict accidently finds a 50 percent person, we usually won't last more than a few weeks because we aren't a match.

People who can carry only 25 percent of relationships have qualities that are very seductive. They might be playful, charismatic, fun, sensuous, all those things that a serious, hard-working 75 percenter might find very appealing. People who carry 75 percent of relationships are also attractive. They seem very stable, responsible, and hard-working.

One would think that all addicts would be 25 percent people, and all co-addicts 75 percent people, but this assumption isn't always true. Usually areas of overresponsibility and underresponsibility occur in addicts and in co-addicts. Many alcoholics or sex addicts, for example, are workaholic overachievers, or have other compulsive outlets which may *look like* overresponsibility but are actually only compulsive outlets for the overload of anxiety caused by the addiction cycle. (See chapter nine). Many co-addicts have traits that make them appear irresponsible—they spend too much money or suffer an eating disorder that preoccupies them.

The bottom line that couples need to understand is that the practicing addict's primary relationship is with his addiction, and he will carry fewer and fewer responsibilities of marriage, parenthood, and finances as the addiction progresses.

The process of a spouse becoming entangled in addiction is powerful and sneaky at the same time. A wife who is asked, and then pressured, into sexual acts that trouble her, in order to satisfy her husband's sexual addiction, feels used and ashamed. Worse yet, she has to deal with a spouse who believes his sexual "needs" are valid and normal and who blames and judges her for not "loving" him enough. Not understanding sexual addiction and being a 75 percenter she believes the accusations, and she shoulders more responsibility and swallows more pain.

The relationship crisis and damage done to any family is in the extremes of over- and under-functioning that come with addiction and seem such a normal part of relationships. If you marry someone for better or worse, you forgive, and tend, you compromise and change—isn't that what married people do? Without knowing it, you are trapped in a downward spiral, accepting more and more responsibility and giving up more and more of yourself to your spouse's addiction. The more a sex addiction robs you of your marriage, the more pain and responsibility you will be forced to shoulder, and the more you will be moved to an extreme. Children sense and respond to the extremes; they also move to extremes so they can cope, as Jennie did, becoming a "wife" to her father. In the extremes is the perpetuation of dysfunctional family systems as our children leave home in search of someone to care for or who will care for them — fertile soil for addiction.

A SKETCH OF THE ADDICT

What mechanism in a sex addict's mind can allow him to go
out to dinner with his wife to celebrate their wedding anni-
versary, drop her off at home, and go cruising downtown to
find a male prostitute? He gets up the next morning and yells
at his child for lying, works hard all day, stops at a triple-X
movie to masturbate, and then goes home and provokes a
fight with his wife because she's "ungrateful" for all the extra
time he's put in at work during the past two days—the lie he
told her to cover his absence. What makes such a man tick?

There is a clear and distinct split between the life addicts
believe they live and the life they actually do live. One ele-
ment of this characteristic is the vicious circle of control and
loss of control, with shame at the hub as the driving force.
Fossum and Mason explain this process in their book, *Facing
Shame—Families in Recovery*:

> *The addict's control phase makes the release
> phase more likely and more intense. The intensi-
> fied release phase calls for more control. Shame
> is at the hub of this destructive process, driving
> it, organizing it, and intensifying both
> phases. . . . Each phase in the cycle is a coping
> response to the other.*

Loss of control is the hallmark of any addiction. Loss of
control, or release, for a sex addict can be as simple as not
paying attention at an important meeting because a sexual
fantasy preoccupied his mind. The addict may experience
shame and consequences by being asked an important
question he can't answer, but that he will face when he
switches to the control phase of the cycle, the natural coping
response to the other extreme of release.

Tomorrow this addict "finds himself" in the midst of a
sexual encounter with his secretary. The shame and fear from
his loss of control about this affair maybe intense if he is

early in his addiction and his marriage, and he is driven to the control phase to hide from his shame.

A woman may feel anguished when she realizes that she slept with yet another stranger, but all she can do is move to the other extreme of rigid control once again and fool herself into believing she'll stop. She cannot find a way out of this cycle. Fossum and Mason go on to say, "The control phase feels like a refuge from shame but is actually only a hiding place and covers the shame."

It's important to know that most addicts lose or do not have conscious awareness of feeling guilty or ashamed after the first few times their addiction has driven them to do something they've always believed to be wrong or sick. It's almost as though a cord has been cut to their emotions and instead everything is immediately "run" through their intellect and comes out rationalized, defended, blamed or justified. Claims of guilt and shame for most addicts become manipulations.

Another dimension of the split between the real life and the ideal one is best expressed in the concept of dissociation. A common protective mechanism that protects children who experience sexual abuse allows them to "go somewhere else" in their minds, to dissociate from the present experience while they are being abused. Most sex addicts were sexually abused and deprived as children and became accustomed to this protective mechanism at an early age. This mechanism, which contributed to their survival in childhood, is probably now their worst enemy as adults who need access to the truth about themselves.

A last facet of the split, a real "crazy-maker" for family members, is shame. Stephanie E. writes beautifully about shame in her pamphlet, *Shame Faced*. She says:

> *Shame's most important objective is **to not be exposed**. Most people who are "shame-based" don't know it. They can't. It's slippery. Sometimes it comes on so slowly, you won't know when you*

*started to feel this way. And it is most often
disguised as what it is **not**: irrational white rage,
indifference, the overwhelming need to control,
depression, confusion, flightiness, the obsession
to use, numbness, panic and the need to run.*

Addiction and shame go hand in hand, and sexual trauma
goes with shame. Most sex addicts not only experienced
sexual trauma, but also grew up in families of addicts. Shame
is passed down through the generations; it becomes so
ingrained and hidden in these families that adult children can
simply trust that it's there and get help for it. Unless shame is
resolved, addictions and compulsions will continue.

In presenting themselves as "normal," many sex addicts
come across as grandiose. Tom Clancy's novel *The Cardinal of
the Kremlin* ascribed to the Russians a national tendency to
overdo a lot of things. It reminded me of sex addiction:

*To Russians, who rarely had enough of anything,
"having enough" meant having more than
anyone else—preferably more than everyone
else. . . .People who feel themselves inferior have
a pathological desire to disprove their own
perceptions.*

If we understand that the addict's grandiosity compen-
sates in direct proportion for feelings of worthlessness and
inadequacy, the addict's "front" and behavior come into
clearer focus.

Patrick Carnes says that four core beliefs underlie sex
addicts' behavior, a concept that can help us understand the
evolution of a public self to cope with the world. We couldn't
function with the rawness of these beliefs if we were conscious of them:

- *I am basically a bad, unworthy person.*
- *No one would love me as I am.*

- *My needs are never going to be met if I have to depend on others.*
- *Sex is my most important need.*

A man whose name I've forgotten laid out a helpful model about beliefs, values, attitudes, and behavior in a lecture I once heard. Beliefs. Values. Behavior. Attitudes.

Our beliefs are at the bedrock of who we are as people. If someone walked up to us and asked about our beliefs, we would be hard pressed to come up with an answer, they are so deeply ingrained. A sex addict is certainly not conscious of the beliefs that drive her and her addiction.

Out of our beliefs come our values, which are easier to put into words and describe, unless we are addicted. In this case we profess values we may want for ourselves but are unable to live by. If my bedrock belief about myself is that I am a good person, it would be natural and easy for me to profess values like honesty and kindness and to carry out those values. If my bedrock beliefs about myself are that I am basically a bad, unworthy person and that no one could love me as I am, then I would naturally try to be "someone else" so I could be loved. The behavior caused by my addiction keeps me in a state of shame, and my shame constantly undoes my desire to believe I am a good person.

Out of our values come our attitudes, which are pretty easily observed. If my bedrock belief is that I am a good person and my values are congruent, anyone can tell by my attitude about each and every situation I encounter in my day what is acceptable to me and what is unacceptable. Addicts display attitudes that conflict with the values they profess. A sex addict commonly professes to be a kind, sensitive person, but his attitude about demeaning sexual jokes doesn't fit at all with values like kindness and sensitivity.

Out of our attitudes comes our behavior, which tells all. No matter what values people say they have, if they are addicted or live with an addict, they cannot practice healthy values.

The sex addict may describe altruistic, open-minded, family-oriented values, but watch his or her behavior. You may observe that he is insensitive, out of touch, disloyal, crude, vulgar, or grandiose, all personality traits common to sex addicts.

Only when the addiction progresses to the point where the pain is intense and the losses can't be ignored, only then does the addict seek help. Too often help is not available because sex addiction is not viewed as an addiction, and the addict and the spouse are not treated with compassion. So they continue to put up a front of normalcy to show the world that they are all right, they are a good family. . . .

A SKETCH OF THE CO-ADDICT

It's easy to understand co-sex addicts staying in horrible relationships if you accept the notion that in their heart of hearts they "know" everything wrong in their relationships is their fault, their responsibility to fix. Just as sex addicts are not conscious of their addiction, neither are co-sex addicts conscious of how they are taking responsibility for everything that goes wrong in a relationship. Countless men and women have internalized the signs and symptoms of their spouse's sex addiction: "It must be me." A sex addict flatly denies that her husband saw what he knows he saw. What does he do after that? He may have a tantrum while his wife looks on in disgust or walks away. He can try to engage her in a fight that he is likely to lose, if he can provoke the fight at all. He can spy on her, but that won't help because she can disarm anything he confronts her with. He may know when to stop pushing because she can hurt him worse than he can hurt her.

The spouse of a sex addict may know that his wife is having affairs. But despite his seething sense of betrayal and helplessness, his flurry of behaviors says, "What can I do to make you love and want me?" The spouse of a sex addict may ignore the obvious for the sake of peace, go on a diet to be more attractive, buy a gift to make up, fix favorite meals, engage in humiliating sexual behavior to please her, apologize for accusations, or do any number of other things that reinforce the addict's belief that she is the injured party.

What does a husband do, faced with this losing battle? He loses more and more of himself as the disease progresses. By the time the sex addiction has advanced to the point of serious consequences, spouses are either spending most waking moments consumed by their troubles; medicating themselves with work, pills, alcohol, food, or affairs; spending money; or throwing themselves totally into the addict's and their children's lives.

The beginning of a sex-addicted marriage illustrates the process as dysfunction becomes the norm. Jim is a sex addict newly married to a woman named Terry. She rebelled against her quiet, strict, religious family by falling in love with Jim when she went off to college. He grew up in a family with an alcoholic father who was always gone and a mother who was a quiet peacemaker who grew increasingly sad and bitter as time went on. A man down the street whom the boy respected as a father repeatedly molested Jim, but Jim never told anyone. He began masturbating compulsively as a teenager and had a few same-sex experiences with older boys at a camp he went to during the summer. He also kept these experiences a secret. Jim locked away these experiences and his feelings and carried on a "normal" life. He fell quickly in love with Terry—she understood him and was gentle and sweet as well as sexy.

The wedding was wonderful, after an exciting six-month courtship filled with dancing and romancing. The night after the wedding, Jim stayed caught up in all the excitement of the party, flirted too much with the bridesmaids, and kept asking for "a few more minutes" until Terry was so tired she was in tears. (She told herself she was being selfish.) The sex that night was not what she hoped it would be; it was more for Jim than for Terry. (She told herself it would get better.)

On the honeymoon Jim spent more money than they agreed to spend, and when Terry got angry, they had a fight that ended with Jim buying Terry an expensive gift to "make up." Terry couldn't believe Jim's insensitivity in spending more money, but when she expressed anger, he pouted. So she swallowed her anger and made excuses for Jim's behavior in the spirit of "understanding." Sex the next night wasn't any better for Terry; as a matter of fact, Jim grew more demanding. After an argument the third night, when Jim wanted to go to their room for sex immediately after their fight, Terry refused him. He got even later in the evening by dancing with every woman in the club who would dance with him and became obnoxious with the women who wouldn't. Terry was embarrassed about Jim's behavior but was afraid to leave for fear of what Jim might do and what other people might think. Jim believed he was the injured party, and, in order to restore peace, Terry wound up apologizing for refusing him sex, and then had sex with him. The next day when Terry tried to raise the subject of her embarrassment about his making a fool of himself, she quickly realized that he thought he had been the life of the party.

This brief honeymoon period demonstrates several examples of the destructive spiral that has begun for this couple and will progress until the addiction is named and help is sought. Perhaps the example will enable the reader to understand more sympathetically the dilemma of the addicted family. On the one hand we addicts and co-addicts believe our behavior is "normal" and, in fact, carry on a life that may appear normal until others come close enough to see the day-to-day struggles. On the other hand, we are desperately fighting a losing battle for our selfhood, our relationships, and our children's health and well-being. How do we get out for help and how does help get in to us?

THE FAMILY AS AN ENVIRONMENT

Claudia Black once said, "The magnitude of the alcoholic experience is such that you cannot stay psychologically integrated if you feel your feelings." And surely sex addiction as a family experience is equally, if not more, damaging.

The environment of a sexually addicted family is filled with inconsistencies, painful confrontations, shame, tension, rage, and fear. Fun, loving moments, and gestures of support may also be woven into the family's days, but provide only brief respite from the pain and even make our isolation seem deeper. Many people, especially those who feel blamed or protective of the family, get hung up when others talk about their pain. "Wait a minute," they cry out. "It wasn't that bad! You can't say it was all bad!" Of course there were wonderful times and times when we were reasonably happy and content.

Readers who begin to feel defensive about the pain of these families need to stop a minute. Feeling defensive is perhaps an indication of our pain about being unable to make things okay. No one person is powerful enough to create a healthy family environment, and a family is not powerful enough to overcome an addiction that has not been named or treated.

Every family provides an environment for its members. An environment is the life-giving or life-taking atmosphere that surrounds a family, created by each person's interactions with all the others. When enough interactions are filled with pain, anger, frustration, inconsistency, humiliation, and fear, we become caught up in shame. We do not understand that all these problems stem from our family's struggle against addiction. We experience the pain and the consequences as shame. It is as though the shame were a byproduct or "toxic waste" from the unresolvable pain of each interaction, permeating the environment we live in. If you are not sure you understand what shame feels like, read the following indicators of underlying shame to see if any apply to you.

❯ Do you have a lot of secrets?
❯ Do you think you have to keep up an image?
❯ When someone says, "I need to talk to you," do you panic?
❯ Are you afraid often without good reason?
❯ Do you get defensive often?

▶ Do you get preoccupied and scared and worried when you
  make mistakes?
▶ Are there topics you work hard to avoid and do you feel
  panicky when you think they will be brought up?
▶ When you are "caught" by surprise about something, do
  you experience a flood of shame, flushed face, anxiety,
  rapid heartbeat?
▶ Do you believe other people are entitled to be human, ask
  for help, and make mistakes, but you are not?

Our son unintentionally gave us an example to help
contrast shame-bound family systems and respectful systems.
He recently came home with the kind of acute shame and
embarrassment that only a fifteen-year-old can feel. A
substitute teacher had asked him to stand in front of the class
and debate a topic with another student. Being unprepared,
our son experienced the excruciating equivalent of standing
in front of the class without your clothes on. The class
snickered throughout his entire effort and broke into laughter
as he stumbled to a finish.

This is the type of shameful experience that can happen to
anyone. But in a shame-filled family environment, a child is
unable to deflect this type of embarrassment. He instead
feels judged and condemned. "How damn dumb can you
be?" is the kind of statement he has heard so often at home.
And remarks like this have now contaminated his sense of
self-worth. It is doubtful that a child from such an environment will return home to seek comfort and support. It would
be better to keep his feelings a secret rather than risk further
humiliation and shame. Without the crucial support of
family, the feeling of shame is compounded and deepened.

In a healthy family system, a child has the freedom to feel
whatever he's feeling. When he comes home feeling shamed
(even healthy people feel shame), his family responds with
support and understanding, not humiliation or overprotec-
tion. And, support may include helping the child see how he
may have contributed to the situation, like not being prepared for a debate class. The mechanisms in this family

teach kids how to deal with shame and embarrassment. This environment deepens feelings of mutual respect, self-worth, and trust.

Most adult children of sex addicts can recall many experiences when they were hurt and then secretive about their pain, in order to protect themselves from further vulnerability. We need to hear repeatedly the fact that everyone in an addicted family experiences shame, pain, fear, loneliness, inconsistency, helplessness even as we carry on a "normal life." This collective experience is our family environment. Even though we are all alone together, we are sadly unable to share or draw comfort about that isolation.

CHILDREN CARRY THE LESSONS OF THE FAMILY INTO ADULTHOOD

The children of addicts learn that it is normal to live two lives, and never to allow those two lives to come face-to-face with each other. Children do not see integrity practiced at home, but their families commonly misrepresent the family's double life as integrity and honesty. We grow up saying one thing and doing another. It doesn't occur to us that there is another way to live. We think that everyone goes home to a version of what we know, or if they don't they are unreachable "fairy-tale" people anyway.

Most sex addicts, for example, can present themselves as wonderful, giving, honest, open people, while the addict's spouse and children often experience the addict as selfish, untrustworthy, closed, and self-centered. What do we think and say when we're told, "You're so lucky to have him for a husband (or father)"?

Many people in early recovery say, "If I'm unhealthy, then everyone I know is unhealthy too!" That lament is undoubtedly true, but not because there are no healthy people. Health and dysfunction are not compatible. Health must move away from dysfunction or eventually be overwhelmed. It takes awareness, desire for change, something to work toward, and

a lot of hard work before health can overcome dysfunction.
Later in recovery, we find healthy people and realize that they
were there all along, but not present in our lives. Healthy
people live relatively quiet lives, especially compared to the
intensity of life in a family living with sex addiction.

Children of sex addicts learn to survive in shame and
develop a way of coping in their families and in the outside
world that is as individual to them as their fingerprints. Even
though our way of coping is uniquely ours, what **is** common
in our experience is the problem of sex addiction. Sharing
what we know with others in recovery is an exciting, perhaps
painful, first step: at last we find that we are not alone. As my
dad said, "I finally found birds with feathers like mine."

Sharing becomes powerful when, for example, a child of a
sex addict talks in group the first time about what it was like
sitting in church every Sunday listening to her dad preach,
and then having him in her bedroom that night. Even to say
out loud that we felt scared, ashamed, and wrong all the
time—without knowing why—is a real beginning.

Children developing in sex addiction learn to cope with
and compensate for our shame in the ways we see modeled
for us. Some children model the greediness, "me first," and
the grandiosity seen in the sex addict. Other children become
isolated and lost. Many move compulsively toward an outlet
that makes them feel better, like work, books, alcohol or
drugs, eating, or school activities.

Children incorporate the sex addict's beliefs about himself, as Patrick Carnes says, for these beliefs are the filter for
our parents' interactions with us as children. As Carnes writes
in *Out of the Shadows*, we come to believe that (1) I am
basically a bad, unworthy person (self-image), (2) no one
would love me as I am (relationships), (3) my needs are never
going to be met if I have to depend on others (needs), and
(4) sex is my most important need, (sexuality). A child developing in sex addiction differs from the adult sex addict in one
belief, that sex is his most important need. For the adult
child, that belief translates to the idea that sex is one of the
few known ways to get her needs met, or that sex equals love,

or that sex is the only thing she has to give to people who are more powerful than she.

As adult children of sex addicts, we go from one relationship to the next, or doggedly stay in one destructive relationship. We are living in dysfunction, unaware. We may be conscious of our search to find all the things we wanted and needed and didn't get. Instead, we wind up replicating the same situation we came from, or the other extreme. People and things outside ourselves can't fill those empty places, and we can't relate to healthy people when we do not have health to share.

Adult children of sex addicts need love, but we only know how to get a perversion of love by taking care of others or getting others to take care of us. If we take care of others, if we do a good enough job making someone happy, maybe some of that person's happiness will slop over onto us, and some of our own needs will be met. It is rarely possible for anyone in these families to develop as a person free of shame and able to strike a healthy balance of giving and taking.

Perceiving that a painful life is normal, adult children are sentenced to struggle on until circumstances, an event, or a person intervenes with enough power to alter the course of their lives. For some, that event can seem as simple as recognizing themselves in a book and going to their first Twelve Step meeting. Usually though, we have expended many years of struggle to reach the point where we can find the courage to walk into a room full of strangers for our first Twelve Step meeting.

As a consequence of the misguided view that our troubled lives are normal, we may hate life or feel nothing but emptiness and loneliness. But we defend our way of living to the death because that's how shame works. When we are driven to defend our lives, we don't get help.

Believing that our lives are normal, we don't know that our lives lack integrity. We may work hard to better our condition within the constraints imposed on us, but nothing works because we are not whole people. We may find a marriage, a job, a compulsion of our own, or some other

circumstances to prop us up for a while, but we are in the
same downward spiral we grew up in. Our shame drives us
and we lack the insight, awareness, or motivation to change
because we know only the life we have—survival on the edge.

As adult children, we have children of our own, hoping
and dreaming that they will provide stability for a shaky
relationship and fill the void in us or our spouse. We were not
able to meet those needs for our parents, and our children
cannot meet them for us. So the cycle continues.

Chapter Four

Mistaking Excitement for Satisfaction

A s mentioned in chapter three, Patrick Carnes writes that one of the addict's core beliefs is that sex is the most important need. "Addicts confuse nurturing and sex," Carnes says. "Sexual activity never meets the need for love and care, but continues to be seen as the only avenue to do so."

Excitement, stimulation, and lust, terms used almost interchangeably with sex, become a central theme in many stories told by and about sex addicts. The high and the escape from reality sought from the intense feelings of sex can also be triggered by the intense feelings experienced in power situations, in spending and eating binges, or from any source the addict discovers and cultivates. The elation an addict experiences after winning an impossible business deal is as much a high as the sexual affair he rewards himself with later that night.

When an addict is not "high" he comes too close to his deepening sense of shame, which he experiences as pain or as an intolerable emptiness that must be filled and soothed.

Again, he finds relief in sex, fantasy, masturbation, exposing, starting a fight, spending money, getting drunk, or going to a porno movie.

Jennie and Mike's story illustrates this point well, and it's a story I've heard before. Jennie said, "It took a long time for me to figure out that when my husband wanted sex and I wouldn't give it to him, he would beat up my son Mike. To my husband, sex meant love, and when he didn't get the release or reassurance he needed, he vented his frustration on Mike." Sex addicts must constantly search for the stimulation that takes them to the state of mind which is their addiction.

Below we will look at how this characteristic displays itself in the addict's life, how it impacts the co-addict and the family as an environment, and what the children learn.

THE ADDICT

The pursuit of a relationship, the danger of cruising, the greater danger of being found out, the thrill of power, the excitement of becoming involved in an illicit romance, the intensity of new sex or a new fantasy—all these situations describe the drug of choice for the sex addict. Like any drug, the dose needs to be increased or different combinations tried as tolerance develops. A fantasy wears thin, and the day comes when the fantasy is acted out; before long, the fantasy acted out is not enough and the addict needs more . . . and more. A woman addict progresses from masochistic fantasies to using instruments for sexual stimulation; finally she does physical damage to herself before she seeks treatment.

A young man's addiction progresses to masturbating in a secluded elevator. Until now, he has acted out this scene only in his fantasy. He is charged with excitement about the possibility that the door might open and someone, preferably a man, might see him. He is also painfully aware that the elevator doors may open to a child; he tried to stop himself with this knowledge, but he couldn't. He also worries because his masturbation is compulsive and seems out of his control.

Yet another addict, a young woman, tries to hold on to her husband by "pleasing him." Their early sexual experiences started with pornographic movies before intercourse. Eventually they acted out the scenes of increasingly hardcore films. One night he brings home another woman, who has sex with the wife while her husband masturbates. She refuses sex after this experience, and he starts having sex "all over town." She finally leaves him, but only after he physically abuses their kids.

Excitement for most sex addicts is in the pursuit of a relationship, not in the relationship itself. A study done on college campuses identified 326 steps from the time a man and a woman meet until they have intercourse. Someone who is socially tuned in naturally moves through each of the steps as the relationship evolves. People considered "fresh" skip steps. This social ineptness or inappropriateness is interesting to watch as sex addicts leap over whole flights of steps. The addicts who are charismatic and charged with energy are as isolated in the crowd that gathers around them as the socially inadequate addict who is isolated and alone in her addiction. Neither one is able to have a fulfilling relationship.

Think about the charismatic sex addict at a party. He attracts those who want to be near the intense energy that surrounds him, but the only people who can stand the intensity for long are those who have unhealthy needs and are "willing" to be used by the sex addict in return.

How common is it to hear of a relationship ending once sex occurs? For many sex addicts, the thrill is in the chase. Everything seems new again—a different brand of perfume to smell as she gets in the car, a head of red hair instead of blond, a fresh new body to fantasize over; but how long before it becomes the same old thing? Sometimes only as long as it takes to have sex. After a while, there is no new mystery or excitement, just the same old thing as the day before, and then it's time to move on.

The old version of this was the guy who pursued a woman with every ounce of energy he had until he reached his goal, which was to "sleep with her." All of her friends had warned her, and she believed them until she came up against his seduction, which was everything she ever dreamed romance could be. How crushing, the day after she finally gives in, when she faces the hollow emptiness of "being had."

Lust for power, lust for material belongings, lust for position—gluttonous appetite for anything the senses can appreciate—becomes another source of fuel for the sex addiction. Intimacy with self, God, and others is not possible and therefore is not a source of emotional and spiritual "food" for the sex addict, as it must be and will be in recovery. The sex addict is starving and the only comfort he knows comes from sex and other forms of stimulation. The excitement can come from many sources and situations besides those which are obviously sexual. Compulsive eating, compulsive spending, and compulsive working are common behavior in sex addicts, as well as alcoholism and drug addiction. Golden Valley Health Center in Minneapolis, Minnesota, reports in a national survey of recovering sex addicts that 83 percent identified another addiction besides sex.

The tolerance for stimulation becomes so great that addicts' senses become dulled to subtleties, and they require more of everything to stimulate them. Sex addicts can describe the "dress code," the "costumes" and jewelry and makeup necessary to attract attention. My dad was known for his turquoise jewelry and cowboy hat and boots during the height of his addiction. In Twelve Step recovery groups, flashy dressing gradually or abruptly softens as an addict recovers and becomes willing to stop attracting the attention she lived on during her addiction.

Fantasy is also a reliable source of stimulation and escape in day-to-day life. Recovering addicts come to realize how much of their days they spent in and out of fantasy. In our family, the big joke growing up was that you could stand in front of Dad and sing "The Star Spangled Banner" without getting his attention. He has huge blue eyes that were always far away. Also significant in our home was the noise level, which to this day drives my father nuts but is also directly agitated by the intensity and chaos that surround sex addicts. They often seem to be in the eye of a storm: they are calm, and everyone around them is "hysterical"; they are "sane," and everyone around them looks "crazy."

The progressive nature of addiction can lead addicts into a spiral that includes more danger as their tolerance increases, setting up a need for more stimulation and excitement that usually leads to more dangerous situations.

A man who is desperate not to inflict pain on his family or jeopardize his position in the community finds that cruising a seamy area of town while masturbating is not enough anymore. He is arrested a few weeks later for soliciting a male prostitute.

A woman is obviously disturbed, judging by her physical appearance, and she is constantly in her room masturbating and drifting farther away from the world she used to enjoy. Her family finally hospitalized her.

A teacher's addiction progresses to his having sex with his students and jeopardizing his job. He always swore he would never let things get to this point. We read in the newspapers about such people: a trusted psychiatrist who seduces patients; a priest who tries to seduce a vulnerable young woman who has just finished her AA Fifth Step with him; a female counselor at a battered-women's shelter who takes a young woman home on pass and seduces her.

Life, as the non-addicted person knows it, is steady rolling hills, compared to a sex addict's peaks and valleys. A quiet life is unfamiliar terrain for an addict, a challenge difficult to achieve but one that must be undertaken for recovery to happen.

THE CO-ADDICT

A sex-addict's spouse may have "trained" in her family for marriage to a sex addict. Maybe she was the one who was going to "tame" him. Little did she know that this intense, stormy relationship would lose its fire as the marriage vows were spoken and that he was not capable of commitment. This relationship in retrospect was clearly dangerous to begin with. Why did the co-addict not see what was so clearly visible?

In *Back from Betrayal*, Jennifer Schneider says that the co-addict equates intense feelings with being vital and directed; he equates moderate feelings with boredom or even depression. He's a perfect match for the sex addict.

Most co-addicts come to understand in recovery that the high level of tension found in dysfunctional families has become inextricably interwoven with love, sex, caring, and romance. "The more I hurt when we're apart, the more I must love you" is their slogan.

Asked whether he feels the constant tension he lives in, a co-addict probably would not know the meaning of the question. Tension must mount to crisis proportions before he can identify it. Just as a fish doesn't know what water is, the co-addict growing up in the tension found in dysfunctional homes has never known anything else. To make matters worse, he has taken tension, agitation, and excitement as indicators that he is alive. Understanding the tension levels in their home and relationships is critical for co-addicts in recovery. If it's not understood and accounted for in therapy, each family member tends to keep looking for the intensity—and even creating it unconsciously—to ward off the emptiness and depression.

Many spouses of sex addicts are involved sexually in the addiction. Some co-addicts talk about their spouses' demands for sex ten times a day, although the frequency is not significant. For other co-addicts, dealing with sex four times a week is painful. They may be drawn into progressively abusive and perverse sex as the addict's tolerance increases. Many spouses of sex addicts are finally driven to therapy by the disintegration of their marriages, caused by sexual demands and problems.

The sex addict truly believes his needs and wants deserve to be met and that the problem is the spouse's unwillingness to participate. Some therapists enable the addiction by working as if this problem were a couple issue instead of an addiction, leaving the co-addict more vulnerable than before.

When an alcoholic and her spouse go for counseling, many therapists are enlightened enough to stop therapy and refer the alcoholic to treatment, but awareness of sex addiction is not as common. When one psychologist who is learning about sex addiction and seeing it in his practice raised the issue at a professional conference, the speaker polled the audience for anyone who believed the condition exists; in an audience of more than a hundred psychologists, only two or three raised their hands.

The lifestyle of these co-addicts becomes so woven into the addiction, it almost seems to swallow them up. It is difficult in recovery to sort out who these co-addicts are, apart from their spouses' addiction. Even more thought-provoking is the fact that these couples usually have children. The talk-show hosts who listen to the never-ending tales of sadness rarely ask about the children, but the people living these stories are trying to deal with their families' day-to-day needs.

For co-addicts who do not participate in the sex addiction directly, the sexual and emotional involvement in the relationships slows to a stop almost immediately after the "chase" is over. Many co-addicts describe being left emotionally and sexually almost immediately after the wedding or the honeymoon was over. Co-addicts personalize the rejection and enter a cycle of pain. First they say, "It's me—I'm not attractive; what's wrong with me?" Then they do something to entice and stimulate their spouses, who usually meet the overtures with rejection. At best this ploy fixes the problem only temporarily and leads back to the next phase of the cycle, which spirals into deeper shame and victimization.

A chemical dependency counselor remembers a couple he worked with years ago whose tests indicated radically different levels of interest in sex. As they discussed her "low interest," the woman cried inconsolably, and none of the therapist's questions or explanations helped. The husband's

death years later in a massage parlor suggested the reasons
why he had sat quietly patting his wife's back and how she
might have developed her attitudes. Although the therapist
realizes that he couldn't have known any better back then, he
sometimes still feels the pain of his own ignorance.

The co-addict will be attended to, if not directly, then
indirectly. She intuitively understands that the addiction
feeds on excitement and stimulation. If she can provide
neither, in a romantic or sexual way, then the next best thing
is constant agitation and crises. Many spouses of sex addicts
present one catastrophe after another, or physical and
emotional breakdowns, or problems with children, to the
addict. Sadly, it is the closest they come to anything resembl-
ing intimacy and feelings of caring and involvement. But at
what cost? "I remember thinking things were too quiet," one
woman says, "and worried that he would leave. He couldn't
stand quiet and sameness. I'm embarrassed to say I would
stir something up to keep him around."

Co-addicts suffer more and more from unmet needs and
spiraling shame, which increases their neediness. They find
other satisfactions in their children, eating, spending, working, drinking, and pills. The greater their agitation or chaos,
the more they need compulsive outlets.

Marjorie is one example of this phenomenon. She wondered whether her husband entered treatment for alcoholism
to get her off his back about his affairs. In treatment, his
peers confronted him with sex addiction, but he refused to
look at what seemed obvious. Marjorie shut her mouth and
"settled for his recovery from alcoholism." They have attended their respective AA and Al-Anon Twelve Step programs, he
for three years and she for six. Now Marjorie is plagued with
physical symptoms and bouts of depression and anger. When
she is not in bed, she is working sixteen hours a day.

Her husband, on the other hand, is supposedly tranquil
and pleased with his recovery. After spending them into
bankruptcy, he is presently unemployed, but he sees this as
important learning in his recovery. He wishes Marjorie would

once and for all get off his back about the intimacy and anger crap! He is working as hard as he can. She claims a need to grieve and have answers about the past. He claims a need to put all that behind him; her need to know about his sexual behavior is sick, he says, and he won't participate in her sickness. They have stormy fights and intense peacemaking sessions when she says she will back off and he says he will try even harder.

This couple can experience intimacy or avoid it only in the constant agitation and chaos that blinds them to the nature of their marriage. They both claim to want a healthy relationship, but their energy is wearing thin with their inability to make health happen. Health for this couple probably will not be possible without the exposure and treatment of the sex addiction, their core problem.

THE FAMILY AS AN ENVIRONMENT

Chronic anxiety and tension become a driving force in sex addicts' families, often moving them into chaos. Perhaps the greatest contributor to the anxiety and tension is secrets. As you can imagine, where sex addiction is present, secrets abound. Secrets about affairs, sexual behavior, relationship problems, compulsive behavior, secret alliances between parents and children, all the consequences of the behavior. Even the most basic secrets about who we are as people become dividing forces in these families.

A second factor contributing to the chaos is that nothing is really as it seems. Parents aren't functioning as parents; kids aren't free to be kids; what people say is not what they do: and the way the family is presented to others is worlds away from its reality.

I remember years ago when I first heard a workshop on family roles. I could never figure out why our family didn't have a typical oldest child until the presenter casually said, "Well, I imagine one of your parents was in that spot."

That simple revelation just knocked me over, not because it answered questions about my family, but because it revealed so much about all our families. When we have little opportunity to be kids, we learn little about being parents. And when we finally become parents, we are still hurt, damaged kids, doing our best with what we've got. We take our mighty weapons of survival and face the world, wearing our shiniest parental armor, hoping no one notices that we're just little kids in tin foil suits. Chaotic? You bet, and scary as hell.

The third contributor to the level of anxiety is the sexual energy and tension that is in the atmosphere: like air — we can't see it or feel it, but we are breathing it in every day.

The health and stability in a family is the result of a healthy and stable marriage, of structure and clarity in relationships, and open, free communication. Living in a healthy family would be like being in a house of bright rooms, full of familiar, friendly belongings.

Relief in addicted families comes from taking control of the tension. We can be scared and tense for only so long before we have to find a way to cope. I remember when I was little and had to get shots, I learned to cope with the fear by biting my hand so hard that I was more aware of the pain in my hand than the needle in my arm. This way, I was in control of my pain, which relieved some of the hurt.

One woman described how she controlled the tension in her home: "I lived in fear of my husband for years, and one day I finally couldn't live that way anymore. I got in his face that night and told him I wasn't afraid of him anymore."

What's significant is that she didn't remove herself and her children from the abuse, she just found a way to live in it with more control and less fear. Some people are so afraid that their lovers will leave them that they break off the relationship to stop the anxiety and also remain in control.

Children growing up in sex addiction are so accustomed to the tension they usually don't know it's there, but they need it. High tension is so "normal" in this environment that it might be compared to a thermostat. If we get too cold we turn up the heat; if the tension level we are used to drops, we experience anxiety about the change. We might also experience emptiness, boredom, or the awareness of our unhappy thoughts and feelings, which increases our anxiety. Consciously or unconsciously, we move toward or agitate a crisis, and we return the tension level to a comfortably familiar level.

Typical consequences of the chaos and tension in the marriage and family are job changes, moves, fights, children acting out, physical symptoms and accidents, money problems, and emotional symptoms. As children grow older and the addiction progresses, we see arrests, open conflict, secrets shared inappropriately, and unhealthy alliances between parents and children as the parents need a confidant. We see sexual acting out by the children. While these consequences are symptomatic of the tension and the progression of the sex addiction, they are also necessary to stabilize and maintain. We live in this vicious cycle that worsens with the addiction. As the kids leave home and marry, they move toward mates whose anxiety and tension match their own, so the cycle worsens with each generation.

Power, money, lust for material things, and the constant maneuvering and manipulation that goes along with those obsessions are also part of the family environment. When either parent is caught up in the lust for possessions or compulsive spending, the children typically exhibit the same or the other extreme as they grow up. A "me first!" environment exists. In my times of selfishness, I like to sing, "The more I get, the more I want and the less I can do without!"

CHILDHOOD LESSONS PERSIST IN ADULT LIVES

The relationships that matter the most are those we can't have. Some of us are "trained" by the sex addiction to relentlessly pursue stimulation. We consciously or unconsciously look for intensity and danger and excitement when we look

for mates. The problem with dangerous or intense relationships is that the only substance for the relationship is the
intensity; when it wears off we have nothing.

I had a friend before I went to treatment who was so
exotic and wonderful that most of the men she met came
under her spell. Looking back, I can see that her whole being
exuded sex. I remember being horrified by a few of her
boyfriends who beat her up. She would find these gorgeous
men who were dependent babies and drive them crazy by
playing games with their heads. It didn't matter how different
the men seemed, they would eventually fight with her and hit
her. Maybe she gave them another chance, or maybe she
moved on to the next one. Even when she was beaten, she
always seemed in control.

I remember thinking she had it all! Once during this
insanity we were sitting in a bar when she coined the phrase
"the relentless pursuit of the perfect man!" She had grown up
in an abusive home and was the most aggressive personality
of three kids, the one who took care of the others. The
intensity and excitement that surrounded this woman were
born out of sadness, fear, and abuse.

What such adult children as my friend *can* have is not
exciting. What is exciting is always just beyond their reach.
For years I watched unhealthy women being attracted like
flies to my unavailable but dependent brothers, who treated
women poorly. Before we went to treatment, my brothers said
degrading things about these women, and I listened and
laughed. I knew I was uncomfortable, but my brothers were
important, while I was not, and I was just grateful they were
paying attention to me. Fortunately, my brothers are in recovery now and, after several dangerous close calls, one of them
married a woman who is now my best friend. A big moment
in my recovery was finding out that I could confront or leave
the sexual jokes or inappropriate talk that can be so rampant
in treatment and in some gathering places of recovering
people. I always thought I had to put up with it.

Other adult children of sex addicts may be so frightened
by the possibility of rejection that they look for "safe" people

rather than the "exciting" ones, men or women we think we can control and manipulate, who won't reject or hurt us. The problem with these relationships is that we invariably look at these "safe" people as our inferiors or we couldn't consciously control and manipulate them. These relationships are quickly used up and move into the boredom we find intolerable, or move into the heated intensity of the stormy marriage we were trying to avoid in the first place. No matter which way the child of a sex addict turns, he reaches the same level, if not the same kind, of intensity he grew up in.

The high tolerance for tension we take into adulthood comes from two areas of dysfunction in sex-addicted families. First, we have become accustomed to the excitement and stimulation that surrounds the sex addiction. The second area of dysfunction that leads to turmoil comes from developing in a family where nothing is as it seems, which means there is no safety. This dysfunction is also common to alcoholic families.

When family life is unpredictable, filled with pain that is never resolved, scarred by explosions that make no sense, when we are fearful and ashamed from not being safe, we have to adapt, or we can't survive. Children adapt by venting the tension or by shutting down emotionally. We then grow up to become adult children who vent the tension around us or who continue not to recognize the tension because we are still shut down emotionally.

My husband and I had to teach our son something about intense "relationships." He had a habit of getting within inches of his baby nephew's face and bellowing, "YAAAA!" The baby's eyes got huge, and his whole face froze in shock. By the time we put a stop this, our son had conditioned the baby to laugh whenever he raised the baby's intensity to this level.

Now, I don't think the baby will experience any special problems from this overstimulation. The issue was a little simpler. If life teaches an infant that fun starts when his nervous system is wired at 110 volts, what does life feel like at anything less? And what is it like for the people around him? If he dates someone who is relaxed and easy-going, does he recognize her self-comfort or is she "boring"? At what level of intensity in a relationship does his internal meter read "normal"?

People who grew up in sexually dysfunctional families develop a meter that is out of whack. Adults who have developed in this environment are open to a number of problems in relationships. Some adult children are attracted to people who are unavailable and cannot commit. Their partners remain aloof, with an attitude that is often mistaken for confidence and self-assurance. They themselves are likely to be children of dysfunction. As insecure and ego-deficient adults, children of sex addicts are drawn to people who seem able to fill the emptiness inside with the kind of stimulation that has come to seem normal.

Relationships like these are characterized by the game of "catch me if you can." The adult child replays her years of living with the sexually addicted and unavailable parent, trying to please, believing that if she tries hard enough, she will receive the love and fulfillment that she lacks.

CHARLIE'S STORY

Charlie is a twenty-eight-year-old lab technician who has been recovering from drug and alcohol dependency for five years. During his recovery, Charlie realized that his father had had a number of affairs in the past. After he discovered Adult Children of Sexaholics, this is what he said:

"I'll never forget the first time I understood what it was to be a child of a sexaholic. A couple of years ago I had a deep crush on a red-haired girl who worked in the same hospital. I was a few years into recovery from my alcoholism and was beginning to feel assertive and ready for relationships.

"After months of fantasizing about this girl, I finally worked up the courage to ask her out. I'm not sure whether I was more afraid she would say yes or no, but say yes she did, and if I was sweating before, I was dripping buckets now. Where would we go? What would we do? What would we talk about? Should I bring her flowers or would she think I was a geek? I was so uptight I could barely talk.

"We met for dinner and planned to go to a late movie. The fantasy started to crumble in the first half-hour. She complained that she never went out this early and mainly went to booze parties. She talked about how funny people were when they were drunk, how much she enjoyed driving them home and coming in late. She didn't realize it, but she was hanging around my old crowd. I knew them better than she did! The movie was occasionally interrupted with long, drawn-out sighs of boredom. I'm sure we were both quite relieved when the date ended. Another fantasy down the tubes.

"I can't tell you how frustrated I was. I really started to get angry because this wasn't the first time it had happened like this. I didn't have drop dead looks, but mothers didn't hide their kids when I walked by. I didn't drink or do drugs, had a good job, paid my bills, told the truth, and I was a nice guy. But, if all of that were true, how come I was having so much trouble with my dates?

"I had to spend a lot of time looking honestly at the truth. The fact was that I was mostly interested in looks, and if the truth were known, in a woman's unhealthy characteristics as well. Since we worked in the same hospital, I soon found out that my date's night life was infamous. Without hearing about it beforehand, I had been attracted to her character at an unconscious level. I began to see that this had been a pattern all my life. I was always getting involved with women who seemed 'exciting,' but the relationships never came to anything. I was looking for chaotic women who provided excitement but no commitment.

"I had to take my first painful look at my need for such harmful intensity. For the first time, I had to admit out loud that my dad had been having affairs for years, and it was never acknowledged by anyone in the family. My folks commonly had late-night, under-their-breath screaming and crying fights that everyone 'ignored.' My dad could say 'good morning' to a woman and make it sound like an invitation to sex.

"Every time we went out in public, we boys were given grooming inspections. To my dad, a relationship was a question of whether people were attracted to you. Even now he's obsessed for hours if someone doesn't seem to like him; to me, those people don't seem really to be rejecting him, but they just weren't making the intense connections that make him feel comfortable. I realized that this was a part of life as a family member of sex addiction. Our house ran on tension, and I just naturally looked for it in order to feel complete."

Like many other adult children of sex addicts, Charlie learned to require high levels of excitement from the relationships around him. In talking to his parents, he learned that the warmth and happiness of their marriage disappeared soon after the wedding. His father was seductive with women. His mother got angry. They fought about it and made up. As the years went on, his father progressed to actual affairs, his mother became despondent, and the faltering energy of the marriage decayed into an unhappy separation into different bedrooms.

Every dysfunction has patterns of survival behavior that "work," but not forever. A relationship is a living and dynamic situation that moves in one direction or another. When I was single, a friend offered me the simplest explanation of marriage I ever heard—you either work at making it fail or you work at making it succeed. Failing doesn't always mean a divorce. Many marriages are just like the one Charlie's parents had during the active sex addiction. They fall into a pattern of interacting that keeps repeating itself. If you had asked them, they would have said they "got along" and even loved each other. But the sex addiction victimized the whole family to the point of spiritual death.

Remember the old description of alcoholism—chronic, progressive, and fatal? The effects of sex addiction on the whole family is much the same. While it may not always be physically fatal (but sometimes it is), without the warmth and growth of intimacy, a spiritual disintegration into shame is inevitable. And shame is death to the individual.

The core of these children, the place where self-esteem and competence should be developing, is so filled with shame that it is inaccessible to relationships. AA and Al-Anon sponsors have tried to keep hundreds of newly and not so newly sober people out of destructive relationships and focused on their recovery. Stereotypically, we are fighting with the men to stop preying on new women and fighting with the women to make them see the destructiveness of their choice in men. Despite romantic beliefs to the contrary, a union does not evolve because of our love for one another. When two halves go out looking, they find the illusion of being whole only when they feel intense emotions. Drugs induce such illusions too. These men and women will not feel better and grow as they should unless they stop being in abusive situations as either victim or victimizer. And to live in tension and chaos is punishing and abusive.

Chapter Five

Control

None of the characteristics discussed in this book is particularly unique to sex addiction. All addictions manifest these universal human traits. The real issue is the impact these characteristics have on one's life.
For instance, everyone struggles with control at one time or another. The healthiest human being makes simple control decisions, like whether to have that piece of cheesecake after a filling meal. He'll pay a price for eating it, but the cost may be nothing more than feeling too full, a discomfort that soon passes.

That same decision is not so simple for a compulsive overeater who carries a lifetime of shameful feelings and memories caused by innumerable "failures" to eat reasonably. Eating that piece of cheesecake may mean leaving the company of friends in order to rush home and vomit—one more memory of shame and guilt.

Same situation, different results. Why? Because the first person made a decision to let down his controls, but the second lost that decision-making ability a long time ago. Binges of eating and purging or overeating compulsively are no longer voluntary. On the contrary, they are a release from the incredible stress of fighting for control. What was once a universal human foible is now a disorder.

Loss of control is a primary characteristic of all addictions, but the other side of this coin is preoccupation with control. Fossum and Mason describe the process in *Facing Shame: Families in Recovery*. As any addict experiences a loss of control over his behavior, the resultant shame and guilt creates a need to prevent such behavior from occurring again. Intensifying his efforts to prevent the behavior from recurring, he begins to feel the consequences of his own oppression: fear, stress, guilt, shame, inadequacy, and secrecy. This cycle must and will end in an overwhelming need for relief, and the one sure way to get relief is through the addiction. The cycle is now complete and begins again, resulting in increasingly intensive efforts to control himself.

Control becomes an issue for all addicts and their family members. In such a tense environment, the need for relief is overpowering and irresistible. Compulsive behaviors abound. Though they may not always be addictions, they are as damaging and shame-producing as addiction itself. Overeating, sexual acting out, physical violence, drinking, and drug use are but a few of the outlets in addicted families.

Some members of addicted families exhibit a related behavior, the effort to control circumstances and other people. The addict might be found simultaneously exerting rigid controls over his addicted behavior, manipulating work situations to "set up" a sexual opportunity, and controlling his family to prevent their infringing on his freedom.

THE ADDICT

Control is everything to the addict. Lacking it, she feels threatened. She therefore constantly maneuvers for power and control in order to protect herself. As the ability to control her life collapses because of the disease, the addict expends increased energy trying to govern all areas of her life. As the addiction drives her deeper into the behavior of addiction, she experiences more shame, more fear, and more consequences. Her attempts at control intensify, consuming more energy, time, and resources. Even while she is controlling herself so rigidly, hoping never to experience the loss of control again, she is setting up people and opportunities to satisfy her addiction when she needs release again. Of course, the addict is not even aware that while she hangs on to control for dear life, she is planning to lose control at the same time.

Sex addicts become so ashamed that many are unable to live without rigidly and incessantly controlling themselves and others. Because of this core of shame, sex addicts are cut off from themselves as feeling human beings. The most common difficulty for recovering sex addicts is slowly, painfully learning to feel emotions that have not been filtered through the shame-based need to protect themselves.

Like any group of people, sex addicts have various personalities, but many addicts are as aggressive and controlling with the people they love as they are passively aggressive with the people who intimidate them. Sex addicts judge people unmercifully, but are shattered when others judge them. They may lose control and spend too much money, and then be angry at a spouse who spends five dollars the next day. Sex addicts go wherever and whenever they want to go, but rigidly demand that everyone around them account for every minute and second. They may act loud and obnoxious, and then say they were ashamed of a spouse for the way he looked or laughed.

Certainly at the root of this need for control is the absence of self-love, self-esteem. In *Out of the Shadows*, Patrick Carnes explains that the addict believes at his core that he is basically a bad, unworthy person, and that no one would love him as he is. Some sex addicts are driven by these beliefs to prove themselves, while others isolate themselves from the pain of interacting with a world where they can't hold their own and think they don't deserve anything anyway.

Many sex addicts were sexually abused as children and grew up in very emotionally deprived homes where sex addiction or alcoholism were present. The shame experienced in these families is not merely the message that they are not worthwhile; it is the more chilling belief that they are not worthy of existence. The drive to prove themselves worthy to live, combined with the charisma sex addicts often have, carries many to prominent positions. News stories are common about capable, powerful men and women whose lives are being destroyed by sex addiction and its consequences. Many of these people hold key positions in churches, media, and government.

Many more are famous on the smaller scale of their own hometown. Adult children often say, "My dad wasn't nationally known by any means, but he sure was known and loved in our small town. It just killed me that he was so loved and respected while he was coming into my bedroom every night and having sex with me."

Sex addicts exert a degree of control in their relationships that is directly proportionate to their shame and fear about the addiction they are trying to hide, and the losses that could result if their double lives are exposed.

THE CO-ADDICT

The interaction of a couple in a relationship is similar to the steps in a dance. It is a mistake to think, "How can that incredibly nice man be married to that horrendous woman?" Dysfunctional people are attracted to one another for the "completeness" the other brings to their lives. My "dance" was that of a helpless woman who needed a man whose "dance" was to be big and strong. Maybe the incredibly nice man's dance requires him to do whatever he must in order to keep his "exotic and exciting wife." We certainly do not understand the abuse he puts up with, but perhaps part of his dance is to appear the martyr. As a relationship develops, a couple's dance becomes more complex and uniquely theirs. When we add children to a relationship we begin a family dance.

In our legalistic and moralistic society, we tend to explain abusive relationships with the notion of victim and victimizer. Legally we describe one person as a victim and another as a perpetrator, and in therapy these labels serve to describe a framework for dysfunction. But sometimes these terms cloud the issue with value judgments. A therapist who wishes to help sex addicts and their families must be exquisitely aware of how fine is the line between victim and victimizers. A dysfunctional person is an incomplete person. Every family member is "victimized" by the sex addiction, including the sex addict. Certainly we are all ultimately responsible for what we make of our lives, but we are most capable when we can see the whole picture, including our own part in the dance.

The co-sex addict's dance concerns finding ways to solve the constant problems presented by the addiction in order to stabilize the family and to keep the relationship. Addicts need to believe they are in control of their decisions; their best rationale for acting out their addiction involves blaming someone else. "If you weren't so fat and unattractive . . ." they may say (the charge is usually false), or, "If you attended to my needs, maybe I wouldn't need pornography." The co-addict may not consciously be aware of the devastation resulting from the addict's blaming, but she demonstrates it with her behavior. The next day she might begin a diet or be especially attentive without ever realizing that her actions are a response to the accusations. The sex addict sees the dieting or the attentiveness and uses it to reassure himself of the rightness of his position.

Sex addiction victimizes co-sex addicts as much as it does sex addicts. Co-addicts are also traumatized by their own powerlessness, by demoralizing attempts to find love in their relationships, and probably by a background of family or generational dysfunction. Spouses of sex addicts commonly seem to be trying to "complete" a family assignment, to make whole a person or family that is struggling with an addiction.

In fulfilling a family role like this, a co-sex addict tries to plug the spiritual holes of the addict, fill in the family's relationship gaps, and manage the impressions of the outside world regarding the family. Under the burden of this herculean task, co-sex addicts often feel depressed and helpless, never realizing the incredible amount of energy they expend, trying to control the situation around them.

Another contradiction common to co-sex addicts is the belief that they voluntarily control their behavior, despite years of consequences and pain that demonstrate the opposite fact. We all tend to look at situations as isolated incidents rather than ongoing events in our lives. Co-addicts see the periods between the losses of control not as brief respites, but as proof that they still are controlling their behavior. Who would voluntarily lead a life of such confusion? I remember watching a juggler try to juggle nine balls. It was just a joke— he knew he could never do it. But for the co-sex addict, juggling these impossible situations is a matter of life and death for everyone involved. There can be no rest, only rationalizations about why they haven't been able to do it and why they must continue.

The co-sex addict struggles with control and the need for release, just as the sex addict does. Spouses of sex addicts commonly try to meet their own needs and keep their sanity through overwork, overinvolvement with children, alcohol and drug use, overeating, joining the sex addicts in their addiction, or trying to make themselves die emotionally. Many of them cross the line into an addiction of their own, which results in further chaos and disintegration for their families.

Shame is an important factor in this dynamic of control. In the introduction to Fossum and Mason's *Facing Shame*, Carl Whitaker writes, "Shame occurs when you haven't been able to get away with the 'who' you want people to think you are." Anyone who recognizes his shame will laugh (or cry) about the truth of this light summation of a most painful issue. Shame permeates all addicts' every thought, feeling, and belief about who they are, but especially sex addicts because of the taboos and trauma involved.

The greatest price for the loss of control is probably the triggering of shame. The co-sex addict often is in the dangerous position of "showing the sex addict's shame" in neediness, dress, or mannerisms; in self-disclosure; or through compulsions or confrontations that can't be contained and kept private. Sex addicts get even with spouses who touch their shame or show it to anyone in any way. "Passive-aggressive" is a term spouses often use to describe the sex addict. A co-sex addict will get a little tipsy at a party and say something about her unhappy marriage. Her sex addict husband will make her pay dearly for this betrayal.

The co-sex addicts I've known are profoundly deprived of affection, attention, and caring, particularly because all their needs are sexualized or seen as threats by their addicted spouses. They not only lack this support from the addict, but are cut off from other sources. The sex addicts' needs are so great that they resent what they perceive as a loss of their spouses' time and attention. Life often becomes so miserable then for co-addicts that they cut themselves off from their support.

Another consequence of the sex addiction for the co-addict is tantamount to the enslavement of the sex addict. A woman I know goes from one relationship to the next, all with sexually addicted men. Although she is suffering, she cannot find a man who is not a sex addict, or an alcoholic/sex addict, try as she may. She has become a slave to her own needs and patterns.

Nancy, a beautiful woman in her thirties, is such a co-addict. She has faced overwhelming consequences from her husband's sex addiction. She has had two venereal diseases, confronted his fathering another woman's child, and been abandoned countless times during their eleven-year marriage. Her husband has also bankrupted them with his grandiosity. Nancy has received intervention and treatment for her work addiction and her codependency. She learned about sex addiction when her husband refused to participate in her treatment.

She seems to be so lost in the addiction, she doesn't hear what she herself is saying. She may agree that her husband is a sex addict, but her fear obstructs her acting on that knowledge. She will be alone, she says, and no one will have her. She says he needs her, he says he will stop, he is so sorry, she's his wife, she has a deep belief in God that tells her she cannot leave, she can't rob the children of their father, everyone who knows him is against her because he's such a fine man — and she "loves" him. Nancy's story sounds desperate, but she is certainly not unique.

THE FAMILY AS AN ENVIRONMENT

Addicted families can't afford to feel or express feelings; communication is dangerous and reality does not match the family myth. Survival in addicted families depends on each person's learning her place. An environment where control is so critical to the continuation of an addiction results in everybody's reacting with shame. Everyone is kept busy learning and gathering defenses. Each interaction has the potential to wound.

The more important the interaction, the more the addict's senses are honed to hear threat, particularly if the addict is getting close to losing control of his or her addiction.

The particular addiction must be examined for the inter-actions forming around it to assess their impact. A woman sex addict, for example, needs to take every opportunity to throw up her hands and storm out the door, "justifiably" upset by the way her family treats her. Maybe she can't get her husband to stop being long-suffering and patient, so she needs to "teach" her son to yell and scream at her. All these interactions that overwhelm her family have one goal: to get her out of the house so she can act out her sex addiction.

The struggle for control creates an environment of compe-tition and one-upmanship. Survival of the fittest is the rule in these families. It's hard to tell who are the children and who are the parents because the power games involve the whole family, and the spouse spends so much time in the losing position. Children learn to victimize the parent in the losing position at the same time as the children are hurt by being victimized themselves. Obviously, the environment is filled with angry and hostile overtones, with underlying fear, depression, and hopelessness.

The misuse of power and control in these families results in feelings of hurt that are not expressed. There is no empa-thy or positive recognition for others, because if someone has a success the others would perceive themselves as failures. Usually the competition for what little attention and affection exists is so fierce that the atmosphere is filled with conflict. Lies and manipulations escalate conflict among the kids and win attention from a parent.

The role possibilities in these families are limited to victim and victimizer, to being on top or to being down. The atmosphere is tense and interactions are fraught with poten-tial land mines. Exposing vulnerability is like throwing a lamb to the lions.

A woman named Karen talked insightfully about just such snarled relationships. She found out that her father had kept mistresses when she was about thirteen years old. No one in her family ever talked about it, but they all knew. She says her parents never fought in the open and their home was always rigidly silent. Each of the kids, however, terrorized each other in truly horrible ways. They found out where the others were most vulnerable and did their best to destroy them. Karen hated her sister's growing popularity so much that, when her sister was home sick for a week, Karen started a rumor that she had had an abortion. Karen remembered many stories like this one about each of the four kids, but doesn't know where her parents were while this psychological mayhem was going on nor why nothing was ever said or done. Her mother finally killed herself with a drug overdose.

The atmosphere in sex-addicted families is often so oppressive and chaotic and so charged with tension it is a wonder people survive. In my own work, many more sex addicts' than alcoholics' spouses have attempted suicide or suffered serious depression, "breakdowns," and mental illness. In alcoholic families, people take a greater variety of roles than the severely limited choice of victim-victimizer. I doubt that many true "hero" children emerge in sex-addicted families, because sex addicts need so badly to own sole possession of all the available heroism. Sex addiction is a powerful "crazy maker" for all.

WHAT THE CHILDREN LEARN AND TAKE INTO ADULTHOOD

In this hostile control-or-be-controlled world, children learn the verbal skills necessary to do battle with words for survival. They learn how to win by bullying, if they don't have the verbal skills. If they have neither the verbal skills nor the ability to bully and intimidate, they learn to manipulate or to "go away" by blending into the woodwork or running away.

In a family of victims and victimizers, stereotypes usually govern male and female roles. I remember my mom's telling me, "My God, Barbara, with the potential you have, you could marry a lawyer!" Granted, the conversation we were having was about the "losers" I kept picking and marrying. I don't think that in my family, however, making it on your own was an option for women. It has been only recently that my mother has shucked that burden handed down to her by an alcoholic family.

I thought that unless I had a man to take care of me I could not survive. I had to pick men I could control, men I felt safe with, who would treat me like a precious little girl/woman. My first husband treated me like his "little girl," but he was also having affairs with anyone he could get his hands on, hiding pornography, fathering children outside our marriage, and never admitting any of it, despite all the evidence.

I kept picking losers because they were all I could handle. In my kill-or-be-killed world, women were not the dominant species, and "successful" men were too foreign and unreachable. When we do find "successful" men among the dysfunctional group we are usually limited to, often they are mean and frightening. The "dance" we learn is the one that determines who we attract and are attracted to. I learned to be helpless and dependent.

Children lose themselves in enmeshed relationships if they grow up filling a void in their parents' lives. The child needs progressive freedom and support to mature, but this movement away opposes the parents' own need to impede that growth. Parents who are overinvolved with their children out of pain have a tremendous need for love and affection, to be worth something as a parent, perhaps because of unfinished business with their own parents, and the inadequacy of their marriage.

When the addict is underinvolved with the children, the co-addict is usually overinvolved. Many adult children of sex addicts experienced enmeshment with a parent. Often they didn't even know what enmeshment was until they began experiencing the consequences of it. Enmeshment, or the loss of self in relationships with others, is extremely difficult for the adult child to identify, much less to overcome.

The paradox is that one needs a piece of self to find himself or even to know he isn't his own soul's proprietor in the first place.

People who are vulnerable to enmeshment are easily controlled by external forces. They are always monitoring how others think and feel before they act. They commonly confuse their feelings with someone else's. They attribute their own thoughts and feelings to others, who deny them; the confusion is enormous from this projection. They are unable to verbalize their feelings, thoughts, or needs until they know someone else's. If someone starts to cry, they join in the tears. All of these traits indicate enmeshment in relationships.

I learned a great deal about enmeshment and stereotypical roles when I first started dating my present husband, Rick. We worked in the same place, and one day I went into his office, used his scissors, and broke them. I was afraid of what I had done, so I hid them in the bottom of his wastebasket. He came down to my office with the scissors and said, "Barbara, you act like a beaten wife!" This was my first awakening to my role as a victim. I didn't realize that in a healthy relationship I had a right to make a mistake, he had a right to be angry, and we both had the right to the safety of doing either.

Another time I kept accusing my husband of being bored with me after working together all week. He kept denying the charge, but I knew it was true. Finally he said, "I think you're the one who's bored and projecting it onto me!" It was true. Boredom wasn't the right word, but I realized I was feeling anxious about all the time we were spending together, and I mistook my anxiety for his boredom.

Another of my memories is about trying to control the shame I experienced in relationships. I had been sober about four years when Rick and I went to a friend's wedding. We'd been going together for a few months, and this wedding kicked off all my desperate feelings about how I was going to get this guy to marry me. I was afraid that if I couldn't trap him into marrying me, he'd figure out how worthless I was and leave me. I knew these were old, old hurts and fears, and I struggled to contain them. We went to the shopping mall after the wedding and as we were holding hands and walking

he said very gently, "Barb, you don't *have* to be married."
I was flooded with shame that he knew, but we kept talking
and I let go of shame and replaced it with what I think of
as "light."

The most significant realization I had about my vulnerability to enmeshment and control was with my mother. I had
been sober four years and had just made a decision to let my
middle daughter live with her father and stepmother. My
family was in aftercare together following my brother's treatment. I reported my decision to the group, and my mom said,
"Oh Barbie, you must be devastated!" I was immediately
flooded with confusion and feelings of "devastation" about a
decision I was very comfortable with, even though I was
worried sick about my daughter. Tears came to my eyes and I
saw myself in my mind sliding off my chair into a puddle of
devastation on the floor. I pulled myself back up off the floor
in my mind and said, "No, Mom, I feel pretty good about it
right now. I had a hard time making the decision, but I feel
relieved and happy now." Mom then said again, "Oh, but
Barbie, you must be devastated!" Group continued after
neither she nor I would budge. I think my mom was hurt, and
we went through a very tough few years when she kept saying
she didn't even know me anymore. For my part, I was exhil-
arated about the person I was becoming, independent of my
mother's needs, but sometimes scared and wondering where
this new relationship would lead.

My mother was always a strong person, so I never understood that she might not have a fully developed sense of
individuality apart from her children. She always gave me
permission to "let her go," but I finally realized she was
unable to interpret my growing individuality as anything but
rejection of her. Freedom in my family would be taken, not
given. Fortunately, when I got a comfortable distance away
and turned around, she was still there, and we have both
become more free to enjoy each other in ways we never knew
before. Our relationship has actually become more complete
and is filled with new respect.

Chapter Six

The Sexualization of Interactions

In an article about treatment for compulsive sexual behavior, Mark Schwartz, Sc.D., and William S. Brasted, Ph.D., lay clear groundwork for understanding the way interactions are woven with sexual meaning in sex addicts' families:

Sexuality emerges at birth and assumes its biologic function along with breathing, eating, sleeping, drinking and other natural functions. When the unfolding of natural (sexual) function is interrupted by psychosocial insult (i.e., "roadblocks"), sexual dysfunction and deviation frequently occur.

Schwartz and Brasted discuss the impact of family relationships on an individual's sexual development and the resultant ability to handle intimacy throughout life. They go on to say:

*During the formative years of sexual unfolding,
severe sociosexual prohibitions and concomitant
unreasonable and harsh punishment for viola-
tions of these prohibitions, are normative in
western culture and are imposed selectively
through religious, cultural and parental sanc-
tions on childhood and adolescent sexuality.
For this reason sexual dysfunction and sexual
deviation are endemic in our population.*

Carl Whitaker said in a workshop many years ago,
"Children feel one hundred percent responsible for everything
in their families." Sex addiction cannot be "hidden" from
children simply because we are acting out in secrecy. As my
father said, "A sex addict who is acting out sexually with his
or her children is no more lost than a sex addict who is
having affairs. Lost is lost!" The same is true for families.
Addicts and their families mistakenly think that because the
family did not know or see, they were not affected. If I am a
young child of a sex addict and my father spends much of his
time away from home, fighting with my mother, restless and
tense, or lost in preoccupation, I only wonder, "What's wrong
with me?" and "What am I doing wrong?"

Members of such a household view life through filters
developed by the sex addiction. They are forced to do so,
since the sex addiction is primary. Primary means that the
family and the addict do not control the addiction. The
addiction controls the family and the addict.

THE SEX ADDICT

Sex is the drug of choice, so sex pervades every aspect of the
sex addict's interactions. One of the first things my dad said
to me about his sex addiction was, " I didn't dream my
thinking was sexual and that, as a result, all my interactions
were sexual." Dad uses the example of seeing a man drive
into a driveway of a house and assuming that man was going

to his mistress's house for a noontime "quickie." He was surprised to discover that people whose thinking is not sexual see the same man and assume he's going home for lunch.

Certainly sex addicts are not always stumbling around "glassy eyed" waiting to get laid. But the filters through which they see all interactions are lust, greed, power, and control. The addict sees the world through sex-colored glasses. These people can make any ordinary remark or incident seem sexual.

An actress on television describing what it was like to have people always talking to her chest, reminded my husband of Bill, a patient we treated for chemical dependency years before we knew about sexual addiction. There was little sexual involvement between Bill and his wife. He had a history of affairs, compulsive masturbation, emotional estrangement from his children—all classic symptoms of sex addiction. But his most revealing characteristic was the way he sexualized his most ordinary interactions with women. I watched the way Bill said good-bye to other patients. Since he was a large man, he loomed over the other men, staring unblinkingly into their eyes before he dismissed them, all the time being unfailingly polite. He stood even closer as he talked to the women, constantly sweeping his eyes up and down their bodies, occasionally lingering on their breasts, seizing their gaze long enough to seal the bond between them. It was absolutely mesmerizing, and the routine was the same with every woman. In fairness to Bill, he was completely unaware of this behavior. He didn't know that his thinking and therefore his interactions were sexualized.

The reactions around him were equally fascinating. Men either followed Bill or stayed away from him. Although he was a very likable man, he had no close male friends on the unit. The women in the farewell ceremony either danced uncomfortably in his tightening noose, looking for a way out, or tended to move toward this charismatic man. These are not opposite behaviors, but rather two sides of the same coin.

Bill is a good example of sexualized interactions because he constantly sent out sexual messages and read the results, and this was a lifelong habit, a means to carry on all his relationships, male or female. In this way, he measured how he was doing and maintained some level of contact with people around him. You could look at a person like Bill and almost read his thoughts: I wonder if this person likes me? Does she find me attractive? She doesn't seem to want to talk, I wonder what's going on with her? God, nice tits, I bet she works out. I'll ask her, maybe she'll be flattered and see what a nice guy I am. She's smiling — God, I bet she's a great lay.

The signals that all sex addicts send and receive are filtered through a screen that originates in shame and the pseudoselves that help them survive. If we believe we are inadequate, we value power and control. If we believe sex is our most important need, we value the vehicles for our sexual pleasures: "free love," "open marriage," "fun," "living fully," and so on. If we believe we can't count on others to meet our needs, our attitudes are "take all you can from life," "get while the getting is good," and "make sure we get our share."

A meeting at work with an attractive man or woman is seen through the sex addict's filter. He interprets innocent gestures and dialogue according to his needs. As the addiction progresses, it interferes with, or endangers his job as he progresses to "hitting on" these sometimes unsuspecting folks.

A meeting with a boss is seen through a power filter, and as the addiction progresses and he is more driven to prove himself, he becomes more and more difficult to deal with.

Many spouses of sex addicts express sadness and anger about not being able to ask for affection or just to be held without the gesture's turning into sex. A woman in therapy cried as she confronted her husband about the evening her father died when she needed so badly to be held. Her husband kept attempting to move into sex acts and became enraged and walked out on her when she continued to resist his advances.

The following diagram illustrates how these filters work:

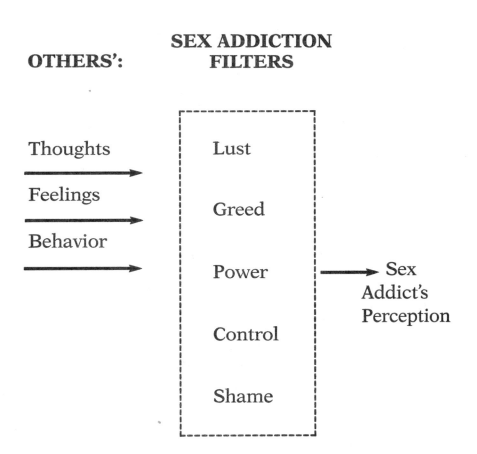

Filter sexualizes thoughts, feelings, and needs of self and others.

At church or work or school, people hug and touch, harmless interactions which the sex addict reads through her filter and interprets as sexual innuendo. As the addiction progresses, more of the people who sense it and are not vulnerable, avoid the addict's hugs. More of the church members who *are* vulnerable, usually because of addiction in their families, are forming a group which can get out of control. I've often heard of subgroups forming this way in churches and turning into a catastrophic group-sex or spouse-swapping experience. Too often a minister's sex addiction is an integral part of this scenario.

Many sex addicts are unconsciously drawn to professions that they hope will help them control or understand them-selves. Priests, ministers, psychologists, psychiatrists, and other caregivers are intensely vulnerable if driven or drawn to these professions by sexual addiction in their lives or their birth families.

Once the addict stops sexually acting out, the next great challenge is exposing the filters, the sexual thinking, and learning for the first time how to respond appropriately in interactions. My dad has a great reminder helpful to any person new to recovery: "First thought, second thought." In early recovery particularly, we are flooded with "old thoughts." "First thought, second thought" means we are never responsible for our first thought because we are human. We are responsible for our second thought, however, which is where recovery comes in. Too often, recovering people judge themselves unmercifully for "sick" thoughts; they try to control their thinking, which only feeds them back into their disease. The addict becomes so worn down by attempts to control, he inevitably loses control and relapses, trapped again in the cycle of control and release.

We have no control over our first thoughts, but we are in charge of our second thoughts. That understanding puts our task in human perspective. My first thought if I am a sex addict is, "How can I get away from work to go to that XXX-rated movie?" If I recognize my first thought, which is the work of recovery, my second thought is either, "I'd better call my SA sponsor or figure out what's going on with me" (recovery), or "I might as well go because I sure won't get any attention at home" (non-recovery). I am responsible to choose recovery.

Sex addicts who admit addiction and are willing to change need treatment in a well-established program. If treatment is not possible, they need the power of a group of recovering sex addicts who will work with them. I've watched several sex addicts who had uncovered their addiction further harm themselves and everyone around them because they lacked the support of peers and professionals who understood the condition.

One woman is ready to leave her community because her husband thinks his recovery requires him to tell anyone who will listen the most intimate details of his recently admitted sex addiction. He refuses treatment and refuses to join a group. He says that he stopped the sexual behavior he was practicing in his marriage, read a book he likes, and is giving "testimony" to his addiction. That, he says, is recovery. His testimony is very inappropriate, but he is oblivious to that fact. After enough rejection or confrontation by healthy people, or after enough unhealthy attention from unhealthy people, he will relapse or need treatment. Stopping the sexual behavior is not enough; he is still practicing his addiction because all the filters sexualize his interactions with everyone around him.

INCEST

Sex addicts often act out with their children. When the addict admits incest, he usually feels relief that the secret is out, and an almost childlike need for reassurance that he presents as shame. The real shame and pain, however, take time and therapy to reach. Common during the initial sessions after admitting incest, the addict says and believes his seven-year-old child wanted the sex and liked it. Some sex addicts believe they were seduced by their early adolescent children. Some believe that, if the child kept the sex a secret, the silence meant that the child wanted the sex to continue. Sex addicts commonly lash out about their needs not being met if they feel "pushed" or intimidated by a relative's anger about the incest. Responsibility takes time and recovery.

Brasted and Schwartz stress the importance of the therapist's understanding how the sex addict's mind works. It's difficult to face a situation where a father molested his baby daughter without thinking, "My God, how could this happen?" I will never forget participating in a family therapy group with a father who had been incestuous with his four-year-old child from infancy on. The courage this mother and this father showed by coming to group week after week to grieve, heal, and learn to parent their child was nothing short of a miracle. I remember wondering at the faulty thinking that had kept this man from knowing the damage he had been doing. I watched his pain as he gradually recognized that his daughter's fear of him and her "night terrors" were connected to his abuse, and I realized that this was a new awareness for him, six months into his therapy. I saw his anger turn to shame when he was confronted for wanting to leave the group when his daughter wouldn't go to him. His childish desire to get even with a four-year-old for "rejecting" him turned into a new awareness about being responsible as a father. People who have sex with children or who demonstrate deviance are not easily viewed with compassion or understanding. We need to see these addicts and their families as being no less and perhaps no more lost than the sex addict whose aberration is extramarital affairs, pornography, and masturbation.

Even the physical and emotional abuse in sexually addicted families has sexual overtones. It's common for the sex-addicted parent to make children, even adolescents, take down their pants for "spankings," to storm into their rooms or the bathroom when they are undressed, to call them names like sluts, whores, or pricks. Children often sense voyeurism or sadistic satisfaction from one of the parents.

Jennie remembers, "My mother would brush my hair and fix my hair until I had little bloody gouges in my scalp. The whole time she ranted and raved about men and what they wanted from you and the sex they demanded."

THE CO-SEX ADDICT

The story Leslie tells about living in a sex-addicted marriage is so common that many women and men will recognize themselves. Her account illustrates the way every interaction with a sex addict passes through filters of misunderstanding that distort reality and sexualize family life. Leslie lives in a big city where she used to have a full life of work, friends, and church activities but in her marriage to a sex addict, she has cut herself off from everything but work and children. She has been desperate about her marriage and wants to leave her husband.

Talking to a group of friends after an Emotions Anonymous meeting, she said:

> *I think being married to a sex addict is much harder than if he were a raging alcoholic. I can talk to some of you about his affairs and his behavior, and you understand that most of what's happening relates to the sex addiction, and you don't blame me. Most people I've talked to over the years have said things that implied I wasn't a "good enough" wife or "good enough" in bed, or he wouldn't be going elsewhere, and he would be happier at home with me and the kids.*

> *I know him. I know there are more affairs than those I've caught him at. I know when he's done something he shouldn't because he gets angry and aggressive at home, as if he has to shove his guilt or remorse or whatever sex addicts feel off onto someone else. If he's not acting out sexually*

*or setting something up, he's spending money,
looking for action or feeling depressed and
expecting me to bring him out of it.*

*The only time he's nice to me is when other
people are around. He expects me to respond to
his phoniness and gets angry and sulks if I don't.
I know the thing that drives him nuts is my
weight and my spending money, and I think that
explains a lot about why I hang on to this weight
and spend money. He never touches me or does
anything for me without an expectation that he
will get something back. He's very judgmental of
other husbands and fathers, whom I see as pretty
normal and responsible. He criticizes the most
peculiar small things but then doesn't see that he
himself is a verbally abusive and sometimes
physically abusive husband and father. He
encourages the kids to keep secrets from me and
plays the victim when I get angry. His best
defense is a good offense. He went to therapy
once and had the therapist so buffaloed by his
bullshit and ability to present himself well that
they brought me into therapy and confronted me
about my weight and about not being a good
wife. He works incredibly hard to keep up an
image at work and in the community and the
result gets back to where we started all this. If
they know about his flirting or his affairs, people
think I'm a bitch and wonder what I'm not doing
to keep him happy at home and in bed.*

Leslie hasn't been able to find recovery as a co-sex addict
apart from her "detached awareness" about what is happening. She knows she's becoming more and more depressed and
suspects her depression is responsible for her inability to
"bottom-line" her husband about going into recovery. She

says one day everything will probably come together in such a way that she and the kids will simply be gone when he gets home.

We could go back through each interaction this man has had with Leslie and everyone else. We could even identify the filters—sex, lust, greed, power, control, and so on. More important, because they're harder to recognize, are the changes in Leslie. Her reactions and behaviors are different, but the filters of sex addiction are in operation for her and for their children.

Most married women sex addicts express their addiction outside their marriage, through affairs, group sex, prostitution, dangerous pick-ups, and so on. Their co-addict husbands experience a pattern similar to the one Leslie describes. They could almost tell you where their wives were in the cycle of setting up their next sexual binge, carrying it out, being caught up in the shame of it, getting themselves "in control," and starting all over again. One husband said, "I dreaded the fight I knew was coming. It was always the way she got herself out of the house, and I couldn't avoid it no matter what I did." Another man said, "She always knew exactly what I needed to hear when everything blew. I was so vulnerable about the kids, and if she couldn't win me over with tears and promises, she threatened to take the kids because moms always got the kids. Some nights I just put my head down on the table and cried from frustration."

Sex addicts commonly bring home diseases to their spouses and then blame them. Co-addicts are used to being accused of everything the sex addict is doing. It's typical to be called too fat, too thin, too ugly, too pure, too frigid, too needy, too motherly, too fatherly, too cold, too demanding, too possessive, too uncaring and every other possible thing to excuse the sex addict's addiction. The problem is that the co-sex addict takes action on these accusations and in taking action accepts responsibility.

A recovering co-addict can cite a long list of her attempts to change the addict—everything from making the addict take the children with him wherever he went to starving herself so he'd think she was losing weight.

Co-addicts who are more directly involved in the addiction are caught up in the same vicious cycle of control and release that determines the addict's pattern. Co-addicts commonly suffer diseases and become suicidal about the progressively "disgusting" things they are being asked to participate in.

THE FAMILY AS AN ENVIRONMENT

Where sex addiction is present, every negative, destructive aspect of our society's inability to handle sex comes into play. Cultural, familial, and religious background interact with the sex addiction to bring this issue into the forefront of the family's daily life. Jennie remembers that her family were "so strongly religious the girls were called sluts and whores by their parents for wearing pants or shorts."

If an addiction is like the proverbial elephant in the living room, then the elephant in the sex addict's home is sex. The secrets are about sex, the tensions are about sex, the fear and the anxiety are about sex, the consequences are about sex, and all these messages are clearly transmitted to the children, who act on them and act them out.

In my family, there was no incest, so how come I identified so much more with the incest families I worked with than with the alcoholic families? Because similar feelings, thoughts, relationships, and consequences were occurring, except the sexual acting out happened away from the family. "Covert incest" is a term often used to describe interactions in families where incest is not taking place, but the emotional enmeshment and unhealthy alliances between a parent and a child result in relationship problems for children that resemble the problems of incest survivors. When sexual abuse was a problem in previous generations, parents are vulnerable to these family patterns because of the boundary problems they bring into marriage. Too much can be made of "emotional incest," and I think this term is too loaded to be used except with great caution. Someone else might say that "sex addiction" is too loaded a term to be helpful, but I think an addiction framework and adult-child concepts are the most helpful thing that could ever happen to families. Sex addiction is rampant, and those who suffer from it are isolated because sex is so difficult to deal with.

In therapy, some people describe physical abuse, emotional and verbal abuse, and enmeshment with a parent that are laden with such unhealthy sexual "vibrations" that the outcomes for the children are similar to those of classic incest. In these instances, the descriptive term "covertly incestuous" applies. We use this term carefully, however, since it is so loaded with meaning it can harm more than help. We also see a tendency to misuse and overuse this term.

A family might be totally unaware of the sex addiction because it is acted out through affairs, voyeurism, cruising, hiring prostitutes, and in adult movies and bookstores. The family might have to "clean up" one or two or even ten incidents, but the whole picture doesn't come together for them.

In another family, sex addiction is played out through incest as well as some of the ways above. This family does not have access to the whole picture either, because the incest destroys the language of self and the family's ability to talk about anything that matters. It's common for a woman to talk about the incest in her family and wonder whether the same thing happened to her sisters. The fact that the sexual acting out is obvious doesn't mean that the kids are aware when they need to be that sex addiction is a problem in the family.

These two hypothetical families do share experiences: inappropriate nudity; calling children or siblings whores and sluts; encouraging boys to be "studs"; making jokes about everyone's sexuality; and giving up thoughts, feelings, possessions, and even bodies to any invasion.

This disturbance may be chaotically obvious or very subtle, depending on the family's style of interaction. Many boys and girls learn the subtle but powerful message that

women are for sex and for caretaking, and that men are for
sex and being taken care of. Many children of sex addicts act
out sexually from the time they are very small.

Julia, for example, remembers that her dad abandoned
the family when she was four years old and left the kids with
a mother who was emotionally unstable. Julia was a compulsive masturbator for as long as she remembers. She masturbated at school, in church, at play, anywhere and anytime.
The fact that nobody ever tried to help her or intervene in her
little life when she was so obviously hurting bespeaks our
society's inability to cope with sexual issues.

Another woman, Megan, remembers:

> *I had a friend when I was seven or eight who
> was so incredibly abusive and destructive that I
> can't imagine what was going on in that family.
> She was my first and only experience with sado-
> masochism—and we were seven years old! Her
> house was always quiet like a church, and she
> had beautiful things—I think she was an only
> child. My dad was a sex addict, and there was a
> lot going on in my family that was painful, but I
> didn't know about his affairs until I was in my
> forties. This friend would tie me up and beat me
> until I panicked and cried. We took off all our
> clothes, and once she poured perfume on my
> genitals and it burned so bad I started screaming
> and her mom came in. What was unbelievable is
> that I think her mom saw what we were doing
> and turned around and left. I don't know what
> all happened in this relationship, but looking
> back I can't believe it.*

Of course the consequences of incest are much more
clearly understood now, and at least the information is available in books. Invading a child through sexual assault does
permanent damage—once that boundary we all have, as a
God-given right, is breached, it is totally destroyed. Of course,

these children as adults can grieve, heal, and learn, eventually restoring themselves to their own keeping. But they must learn to set boundaries one interaction at a time. You don't have sex with children and take only a little piece, and they do not repair themselves after you leave.

Beth, who had a wonderful family and lived in a small community, is a case in point. "One night when I was fourteen," she told me, "my dad took me camping and told me he was going to show me his love for me. He had sex with me, and it was the most gentle, sweet, and wonderful experience I've ever had." As Beth explored this incident, she reported that her father had never made a sexual move before or after that day. No one ever discussed or even mentioned this incident again. It was such a wonderful experience that the only harmful consequence was the time she spent in fantasy and preoccupation, wishing for it to happen again. She saw no damage in her family's life, but Beth's children were in terrible shape—one was in treatment for chemical dependency, and the other was a runaway. We were unable to work with this family because Beth became angry and left, taking her children with her.

WHAT THE CHILDREN LEARN AND TAKE INTO ADULTHOOD

Children of sex addicts learn to view the world through filters of sex, lust, power, greed. . . . It's no wonder they themselves often look like sex addicts. Many therapists see shame at the root of compulsivity and cite the importance of intervention to stop the behavior before working down to the underlying cause. Shame is at the bottom of adult children's personalities. Compulsivity is a natural outcome of shame and of sexualized interactions that perpetuate and compound the shame. Adult children may have a primary addiction or two that require treatment, but it is critical to address the sexualization of their interactions and trace it back to generational sex addiction. Too many professionals expect the sexual behaviors to "go away" in recovery from another addiction like alcoholism or an eating disorder.

Adult children of sex addicts are often so fearful of their needs not being met and so filled with shame that they develop a "me-first" kind of competitive reflex. They can experience compulsive spending, compulsive overeating, and competition for everything with an irritating watchfulness to make sure they get their share.

Children of sex addicts are commonly provocative and seductive. Their dress, hairstyles, makeup, and mannerisms often leave a sexual impression. They might also be compulsive storytellers and liars, seeking the level of stimulation and excitement they've come to need or reacting to shame about their felt inadequacy. In *The Courage to Heal* by Bass and Davis, one woman said, "I lied all the time. I didn't tell lies to get out of trouble. I told them to erase differences, because I felt so weird. I lied to make connections with people."

Another woman, Mickey, found recovery because of the blatant sexualization of her own and her children's behavior and interactions. Mickey decided she needed to get to work on her sex addiction when she kept hearing the feedback that she and her two daughters all came across as extremely seductive. Both girls were promiscuous, and one had been kicked out of two schools for sexual acting out. Therapists kept asking Mickey about a history of incest, but she denied it. Finally, out of desperation, she went to an aunt, pleading for anything she might know. Her aunt sent her away, but the next day invited her back. At her aunt's house, she found her mother. The two sisters talked for the first time about their grandfather and their uncle, who had molested them for many years in childhood. They had tried to go to their parents, who didn't believe them and spanked them for telling such horrible lies.

Mickey began to study the family dynamics of sex addiction as part of her therapy. She and her daughters are working hard to understand and change their distorted vision, passed down the generations to them, through which they've assessed their self-worth and sought out their relationships.

They are in therapy together and doing things like not wearing makeup and committing to celibacy until they are further along. Mom believes she is a sex addict but her daughters are not sure and have not experienced the problems with abstinence that their mom has.

Boys coming from sex addiction display similar attitudes, sometimes the same seductiveness commonly seen with girls and sometimes the other side of the same coin, which is a more aggressive style of behavior. Boys are also promiscuous, using and allowing themselves to be used, but more frequently they sexually harass women and appear to have no values in relationships. Girls and women usually present an illusion of "coyness" or pretenses. Women ACOSAs most often talk about dependent relationships and "needing a man" in their lives. A group of adolescent girls in a halfway house for chemical dependency seized upon a sentence they read in a book: "Girls give sex to get love and boys give love to get sex." These girls thought this was "the most right-on thing they'd ever heard!" For some of these girls, recovery from their chemical dependency will be enough to stop this behavior. For others, especially those who grew up in sex addiction or other sexual dysfunction, this issue will keep undoing their recoveries. They will eventually move into another addiction or marry into a horrible situation until they understand and address their unconscious sexualization of interactions.

Crudeness, grossness, foul sexual language, inappropriate dress, abusiveness, or demeaning attitudes toward women tend to be common issues for men who grew up in sex addiction. Girls and women act out in these aggressive ways less often than their male counterparts.

Children of sex addicts are often promiscuous relationship addicts who use sex to bond a relationship or to create the illusion of intimacy. An affirmation in the pamphlet *Shame Faced*, by Stephanie E., encourages readers to forgive themselves for accepting sex when they wanted love. They do not know another way.

Jennifer bears out this understanding:

*I didn't know my dad was a sex addict yet. I
didn't know there was such a thing. I married my
first husband when I was seventeen after knowing him for three weeks. We were married for
four years. The whole time we were married I
had a giant inferiority complex about sex. He
tolerated sex and I tried harder to get him to love
me and think I was sexy. I went nuts when I
found out from my friends that he'd been having
affairs practically the whole time we were married
and even got someone pregnant when he went
away to National Guard Camp.*

*My second husband was someone I married
when I finally couldn't stand being single anymore. I had been single from August to April and
went through the worst time I'd ever had in
my life! I had two kids, I was twenty-two and
desperate for a man to take care of me. Of course,
at that age the available guys were in college. I
slept with so many jerks hoping Mr. Right would
come out of one of those one-night stands. What
does that tell you about me! I finally tracked
down an old boyfriend I had jilted in high school
and systematically went through the steps to get
him to marry me. He was insanely jealous and I
was so wounded by my life that I got scared of
him, and for the next two miserable years, he
went nuts every time I was gone ten minutes
too long.*

*My life got so bad I was physically abusing my
kids and trying to get some help in a program
called Emotions Anonymous. I called him one
night and said I was going out for coffee with the
group. He was mad, but I did it anyway. I came
home, and he had drunk all the wine we had in
the house, which was only two half bottles. He*

looked ridiculous sitting in that chair with those two empty bottles sitting on the floor. He said, "Who were you out fucking tonight?" All of a sudden I wasn't scared any more. I knew the scared me would have pleaded with him and placated him, but for the first time in two years I didn't want to dignify what he had said with a response. I took a shower, and he ripped the shower curtain down, saying, "What are you doing, washing it off?" That was the end for me.

We still had two horrible years of marriage, every time I had the opportunity, I got in his face before he could get in mine! Sex was woven through all of this. The sex even changed when our relationship did that flip. I don't know how long we would have continued but a friend sat me down and said "This can't go on! This guy is losing it regularly, and you seem to be getting off on the power. Don't you see what it's doing to the kids?!" I left him and had to face what I think I was so scared of. I was searching for a husband again, sleeping around again, and hating myself. Thank God I went to treatment for chemical dependency. I had to face all the shame later though, when I continued looking for someone to take care of me after I got sober. I finally made some changes but they were limited until I found out about the sex addiction in my family. I always knew it was there. Everybody knew about my grandpa and his affairs and my dad's affairs, but nobody was talking about sex addiction and what it does to families. Now it feels like a blessing and a burden to have new information that shows me the work I have to do.

Adult children of sex addicts who have the gift of knowing or suspecting sex addiction in their family can begin their recovery in a framework that makes sense of their problems. Responsibility for change is much easier when we understand the problem in the context of generations of family interactions rather than wondering why we are behaving strangely and why we can't stop. As these people find and treat their addictions, stop the compulsions, resolve the shame, and find different ways to relate to others, they create a new legacy for their children.

Chapter Seven

The Road to Recovery

D r. Walter Lechler once said that the oldest disease known to man is our separateness from God and from each other. We believe that, in its most intimate terms, recovery is the journey back to the God of our understanding, back to that relationship which makes us truly whole again. Being human means we all are recovering; there is a universal need to be whole, a drive to be part of something greater than ourselves.

This spiritual drive is sometimes interrupted by crises or traumas which change the direction of our lives and cause us to lose the way. Feeling the intense fear and loneliness of our lives, we instinctively seek solace in the world around us, too often choosing things that only deepen our pain and despair.

The beauty of suffering is that it sometimes forces us to seek a new way of life that we would not have found without a crisis. Many people never receive help and guidance during their trouble, but that is all the more reason to continue trying to define and understand the human condition. The more we know about the things that keep us lonely and afraid, the more likely it is that help will be there when a crisis occurs.

I went to my first Twelve Step group, because I didn't want to die. It was just that simple. Alcoholism had depleted my life to the point that it had no room for concern about relationships, bills, thinning hair, or any of the other worries that seemed like the luxuries of bored people. I just didn't want to die.

As time went on, I continued my Twelve Step meetings and began to think I might just make it. I developed a desire to survive; in fact, it was a point of pride. I went around carrying my shield of survival in front of me, bashing at anything that got in the way and yelling my war cry of "I'm an alcoholic!" It was energizing and liberating, but something wasn't quite right.

A new feeling began to sneak up on me, quietly, insistently. I began to realize that I wanted really to LIVE, to participate and find out how fulfilling life might be. I saw that deep down I was a scared and lonely person who wanted to belong with the people around me. That's when I first realized that recovery from alcoholism was just a beginning, only a place to start, and the real job was much bigger. My recovery from alcoholism would always be my foundation and road map, but I needed to do more than stay sober. I needed to belong.

Our disease is literally our link to God. It also provides the crisis that begins that journey back. Defining a dysfunction such as sex addiction is important not only to provide a structure for effective treatment, but also to allow thousands the same spiritual awakenings already afforded alcoholics. Many people have suffered from the deadly shame of their undiagnosed, misunderstood diseases, unable to face a loving and lovable God. They were unable to develop warm nurturing relationships with the people around them, felt unworthy to be a part of humanity, and led quiet, desperate lives leading to lonely deaths.

We have a task while we are here. As we begin our journey back to God, we are to develop and learn about that relationship by experiencing it with our brothers and sisters. As people say, "God don't have no grandchildren." There are just His many children, and He's put us here for a reason. He has allowed us a means to glimpse His deep, abiding love, a way to experience the unfathomable love and acceptance He has for all of us. All we need do is reach out for one another and learn to be vulnerable to the God experience He provides. We are on loan to each other.

Chapter Eight

Start at the Beginning

Here I want to begin talking to you, the reader, directly, for each journey begins with the first step, and in this case, it begins with you. If you have found yourself somewhere in this book and want more information on recovery, we hope to offer some suggestions and ideas. But we want you to understand that everyone's recovery is a little different. Books are a wonderful means to inform and stimulate, but they are no substitute for contact with people. This book cannot take the place of a therapy group and Twelve Step participation.

Despite the fact that sex addiction is a relatively new concept in the helping professions, knowledge of this condition is rapidly growing. The new organization, Adult Children of Sexually Dysfunctional Families, is a logical outgrowth of the sex addiction movement, but is in its earliest stages. Help and information is not readily available as yet. The first Twelve Step groups have already begun and in time will spread throughout the country. If you are already in a Twelve Step group or have been through therapy, you are no doubt familiar with recovery concepts. If you have had no previous experience with either, there are many fine books on recovery. In fact, many bookstores have established a separate section on alcoholism and codependency. There you may find books about other dysfunctions as well, such as *A Time to Heal* by Timmen Cermak, M.D. Although his book is about codependency, it is a helpful guide to recovery principles and addresses issues common to many dysfunctions. This chapter is based largely on Dr. Cermak's ideas.

RECOGNITION

It is doubtful that many adult children of sex addicts have been identified as such while they were being treated for a primary addiction of another kind, even if abuse, incest, and other traumas may have been addressed. Because of their boundary issues, children of sex addicts are either such perfect users of the system that they escape detection or they are so distrusting, they cannot tolerate the seeming invasiveness of help. Professionals are rightly hesitant to apply labels such as "sex addict" to family members not present during treatment. Speculating about sex addiction back through other generations of a family is even more difficult.

If you believe sex addiction was present in your family and if the dynamics of sex addiction typify your family experience, complete the chart in this book and find a therapist who works with sex addiction and family dynamics. You will hear about good family-oriented therapists by attending Twelve Step groups, particularly Adult Children of Alcoholics (ACOA) and Codependents Anonymous (CODA).

ASSESSMENT OF ADDICTION

There is a positive side if you have been in treatment or already attend a Twelve Step group for another disorder, even if you have not been identified as an ACOSA. It is important that primary addictions be treated before or during recovery. It is absolutely vital to have clear access to your thoughts and feelings. Drugs and alcohol or food initially may have dulled pain but eventually became a primary source of pain in itself, taking over what ability there was to cope. Any therapy situation raises levels of anxiety and stress; if you were medicating yourself, recovery as a child of a sex addict would be impossible. The beauty is that previous treatment will already have developed your coping skills.

If you have not had previous experience with treatment or a support group, ask for an assessment of addiction by a professional if there is any question in your mind whatsoever. We always encourage professionals to check for addiction as part of an assessment process.

Members of your family may have an addiction. Maybe a family member's addiction is what brought you to the crisis point where you had to do something different in your life. Recovery is difficult in the best of circumstances. When you feel alone, wanting recovery when a spouse or child does not, you probably feel damned if you do and damned if you don't. You have one choice, which is to change your *own* life, fearful of the consequences change will bring in your marriage and relationships. Your other choice is to try and forget you ever read this and the other books you've been reading and "go back to sleep," which you probably can't do.

Your motivation for help will be tested if you find that another family member is addicted. The bottom line is, you can't change anyone but yourself. As you change, your situation will change for the better or it will worsen, forcing more change.

CHANGE AND THE FAMILY

If you choose to enter into a recovery process (therapy and Twelve Step program) while important people in your life do not, their absence will create a gap in your relationship. It is

only natural for the people you love to feel threatened by your
decision, especially if they see you actually following through
by making changes. As family members and friends realize
you are seriously attempting to seek help and to change, they
will find a thousand ways to tell you that they want you back
the way you were. For example, a crisis occurs three Wednes-
days in a row, which just happens to be the night your Adult
Children of Sex Addicts group meets. Or everything you
wanted to see changed in your situation improves for a
period of time, making you doubt yourself and threatening
your fragile hold on recovery. You might hear messages like,
"You've changed, and I don't feel like I know you anymore,"
or "If you loved me . . ."

Be assured that in most situations the people close to you
are afraid. When you've lived in dysfunction all your lives, the
only thing you can count on is the unpredictability of that
dysfunction. Any extraordinary change sends a ripple of fear
through everyone involved. A story from *I Exist, I Need, I'm
Entitled*, by Jacqueline Carey Lair and Walther Lechler, M.D.,
my mother's book, beautifully illustrates the wonderful-awful
process that is change:

> *As we grow up, we are all seeking complete enti-
> tlement to live as we experienced life in the womb
> of our mothers.*
>
> *We had this experience, and it is quite natural
> that we all seek instant pleasure, maximum
> safety, no responsibility, power and this terrific
> feeling of entitlement. Many of us haven't learned
> that we need to work hard, have patience, endure
> frustration in order to regain this experience.*
>
> *We try to build ourselves a nest to give us this
> feeling. We plant our orchard. We get a nice, neat
> house and we furnish it to our taste. We build a
> huge fence around our property. We select our
> relationships. We try to be independent in our*

*supplies. We have our own well. We try to grow
what we need so we are not dependent on others.*

*Sometimes we go up to our attic and look out.
Outside of our fence we see a huge land. Beautiful prairies, rivers, lakes, mountains. We see huge
herds of cattle. We see the noisy cowboys round-
ing up the herds. At night we see their campfires
and hear their songs drifting back to us on the
wind. We don't want to take the risk they take.
They are out there in the wind, the rain, the cold.
We have our fine, protected little nest, our new
artificial womb we have created.
Then one day a crisis comes. A tornado blows
across the prairie and destroys our orchard. Our
fences are flattened; our house is torn from its
foundation.*

*We panic. We feel pain and fear. We feel a terrific
anger that this has happened. Sometimes we
even want to kill ourselves because life has
treated us this way.*

*If we are lucky and don't destroy ourselves, we
step outside of our ruined acres. We do this full
of fear and trepidation. We don't know who this
land belongs to. We feel uneasy and walk carefully, watching for other people, waiting for a
rebuke, a signal that we are intruding. We timidly
approach the campfire of the cowboys we have
watched from our attic all these years. If we are
lucky, they ask us to come and join them. They
give us a plate and share their food with us.*

*Then we begin a timid conversation with these
cowboys. We finally get the courage to ask these
men who this land belongs to.*

*"This land belongs to very wealthy people over
there behind the hill. They have a beautiful house
and orchard and a high fence and we never see
them, but all of this is theirs. Isn't it sad that they
never come out to see their lands? Their lakes,
their mountains, their prairies? All of these cattle
belong to them, too. We work for them. We just
get their orders, though. We have never seen
them."*

*We cannot believe it. They are talking about US!
We own this land and we never knew it!*

*Being the owners of this new land frightens us.
We must accept responsibility now for all that we
own. We feel untrained for this job and we want
to go back and fence up this place that we knew.
Sometimes we do this. We rebuild our fences, but
we can never feel the same again with our new
knowledge. Because life loves us, a second crisis
comes or even a third. Crisis comes until we
accept our ownership.*

*When we assume responsibility for what we are,
we must go into our land and possess it. We
must find the joy and the love that is ours.*

*We must listen to the cowboys and the guardians
of our forest. They did what we didn't do. We owe
them our lives. They can show us the way to stay
out in our land and how to possess it.*

As you persist in your efforts to change and get healthier
and stronger, the gap will widen between you and family
members who are caught up in unhealthy patterns of a lifetime or who have an addiction of their own. The stronger you
get, the better able you will be to encourage your family and
friends toward the help they need. Decide, with the help of

your therapist, when you are strong enough and have enough support to intervene with family members who are caught up in an addiction. Sometimes a crisis will force you to intervene before you are "ready," but try to find the support when you need it. In my family, as of June 1990, my mother has thirteen years of recovery, my younger brothers have eleven years, seven years, and six years. I have ten years, and my father has seven years of recovery. You can imagine what those first years were like for my mother. It's always tough to be the first, but how much worse for no one to recover.

TWELVE STEP GROUPS

It is always important to join a Twelve Step group. There is an old saying for alcoholics that treatment is discovery and AA is recovery. By nature, therapy is meant to be temporary, lasting only as long as is absolutely necessary. But a Twelve Step group is an ongoing source of insight, awareness, awakening and fellowship. Therapy helps us to draw the initial road map, Twelve Step attendance keeps us traveling on the proper route.

If you are interested in finding a Twelve Step group to attend, it might be impossible to find an Adult Children of Sexually Dysfunctional Families meeting. In that case, you might consider groups such as CODA (Codependents Anonymous), ACOA (Adult Children of Alcoholics), or Al-Anon. It should also be mentioned that not all groups such as this are Twelve Step–based. Some are support groups without a specific structure like AA, but offer the same basic help and understanding. If you are already in a Twelve Step group such as AA, continue going and give strong consideration to adding another group that will focus on your relationships.

Obtaining a sponsor is the next important step. A sponsor is generally someone who has been in the program for a while and can lend personal experience and knowledge about the program. It is wise to pick someone you feel comfortable with, and it is always suggested that you choose someone of the same sex or opposite your sexual preference. Perhaps you won't be immediately attracted to a group after your first meeting. It's important to commit yourself to about five meetings to really get a feel for a group. If you still are not interested, try another meeting. Each group has its own personality and style.

If you are interested in starting an ACOSA group, you can get more information by contacting Adult Children of Sexually Dysfunctional Families at the address on page 183.

THERAPY

Although it's doubtful at this time that you will find a therapy group specifically for children of sex addicts, it is possible to find a therapist familiar with sex addiction. It is important to consider therapy for the fallout of living in a sex-addicted family—incest, intimacy problems, shame, compulsive behaviors, relationship difficulties, and the many other problems that need resolution.

Many people are frightened by the idea of seeing a therapist. Perhaps you may feel that only "crazy" people see therapists, such a relationship may seem invasive, or you might feel frightened by the thought of giving over some of the control in your life to another person. All of these concerns are valid and you should pay attention to them. A skilled therapist will also pay attention to these concerns and will be sensitive to your feelings.

When seeking a therapist, consider two possible sources of information in your area. One is peers in your Twelve Step group, and the other is a local resource for codependency therapy, which can recommend professionals familiar with issues related to a childhood in a sex-addicted family. Members of Incest Survivors Anonymous can be a good source for finding a therapist to help you recover from incest.

It should be mentioned that Twelve Step groups have no opinion on outside issues, and the topic of therapy and therapists are not always welcome during meetings. It is suggested that you discuss these issues before or after meetings.

Many people have difficulty with the idea of questioning an authority figure, but it is hoped you can find the means to do so. When you contact a therapist, the first test will be whether you can ask some questions before paying for a session. Most reputable therapists invite questions about their practice and background. If a therapist refuses to talk to you without your first coming in or has a secretary playing middle-man, you might want to consider someone who is not quite so busy.

Following is a list of possible questions to ask:

1. Do you work with addiction and do you recommend Twelve Step programs?
2. Have you ever worked with sexual addiction?
3. Are you experienced in working with sexual trauma (if this is appropriate to your life)? What is your training, education, or background in sexual traumas?
4. Can you tell me something about your style? (For instance, is there physical contact between you and your client? Under what conditions, and toward what goal? Do you mostly listen while I talk, or is there discussion between us? Do you work in group therapy or individually?)
5. What will happen if something comes up that I don't want to talk about?
6. How will you work with my family situation?
7. What are your charges and how do you bill? Is there a sliding scale (reduced charges according to income)?

We recommend that you engage a therapist who believes that addiction is a primary illness. The addiction model provides a clear and useful structure for your recovery. We also strongly recommend that you consider group therapy as the primary approach for your recovery, with individual sessions as needed. You may need several private sessions before you can overcome your fear of trying group therapy. Do what you need to feel safe. Again, you may not find a group composed strictly of children of sex addicts, but usually a codependency therapy group will do very nicely, particularly if your therapist understands sex addiction. Your first session in group therapy may make you feel like the ugly duckling entering a flock of swans. You may feel scared and out of place, but imagine the joy when you see that your feathers are just like theirs. You will find that you are not crazy or alone. If you think you need to start with individual visits, talk it over with your therapist.

You may be more comfortable with a therapist of your own or opposite gender. As a rule of thumb, particularly with sexual traumas, it is a good idea to stick with a same-sex therapist.

Chapter Nine

Breaking the Cycle of Addiction and Family Dysfunction

I f there were a simple way to talk about the circular flow of trouble families are encountering from generations of addiction it would be:

—— Addiction causes family dysfunction
—— Family dysfunction leads to fewer skills for healthy relationships
—— Fewer relationship skills lead to unmet needs
—— More unmet needs lead to more anxiety and frustration
—— The more anxiety the more compulsive outlets we seek
—— The more compulsions we have the more vulnerable we are to addictions
—— Addiction causes family dysfunction
—— And the cycle continues

People wanting to break this chain need help to develop a plan for recovery. Once we have an idea where to begin we need support and teachers. We suggest the simple framework above to help you assess yourself and your family and develop a plan. Each plan should involve exactly enough work—taking into account the needs and the seriousness of the situation—so we are not overwhelmed or scattered in our focus.

For example, I might suspect I am suffering from anxiety because I realize I've become compulsive about work and spending money. Using this framework, I look back and try to identify the needs that I feel have been unmet. Perhaps I am not feeling close to my husband because we've been fighting, and I'm losing my contacts with my friends. Then going back a step, if I do not have the relationship/communication skills to understand, express, negotiate, and solve the problem, I had better get some help. Sometimes the help I need can be as simple as using a healthy friend for a sounding board. Sometime I may need a counselor, sponsor or group to help solve a problem. If I do all this and I am still compulsively working, spending money, and feeling needy and anxious, it may be that problems with my husband and separation from my friends are happening because I am trapped in compulsive spending and working rather than the other way around. Now I can get help to stop spending and working and see if I don't feel better about myself and thus my marriage and my relationships with friends.

We also need to understand that our recoveries are interrelated with the recoveries of people we love. If my husband is actively alcoholic, I can only realize and recover from my own compulsions or addictions. My healthy needs will not be met in an environment where others are actively addicted.

ADDICTION CAUSES FAMILY DYSFUNCTION

I don't think anyone would disagree with this statement. Obviously, the necessary first step in tracing back through the process is to find and name an addiction, if you can.

If I am an alcoholic or drug addict, I won't get well until I'm willing to stop using alcohol and drugs. My recovery begins with me. Just as important for Adult Children beginning recovery is to name an addiction present in a parent— if you are able to do so. To realize that an addiction was responsible for all this unhappiness in your family of origin can be a great relief. We also need to evaluate carefully our present situation to know if someone we are living with is addicted. For example, if I have an addicted child in crisis, I may need my therapist for support to intervene with my child. If I have an alcoholic or sexually addicted husband, wife, or child whose addiction is constantly undermining my attempts at recovery, I will need help to intervene.

Education and support are critical if we are to be convinced that addiction is a primary problem and that we can change. "Primary" means that most of the problems which caused us enough pain to get help will not go away as long as we still live with an active addict. Too many people suffer from the belief that they can change an addict with enough love, discipline, education, guidance, patience, or prayer. My mother came back from treatment and says she felt like she had been shown a beautiful garden that was recovery. She wanted to show us the garden and how beautiful life could be but, because we were all unaware and practicing addictions and compulsions, we were trapped where she had been before treatment. Mom visualized all of us as "in the house shoveling shit." She would try to get us out into the garden and we would all try to get her to come back in and shovel shit with us. We'd get traffic tickets, we'd get arrested, we'd bounce checks, we'd sleep around, we'd come home with some *pretty* scary people, we'd be sorry, we'd say "this time I'll change," we'd do everything else addicts do. Fortunately, my mother was powerful enough to force us, one at a time, into treatment centers, rather than just give in and threaten her own recovery. Treatment for us turned out to be the entrance to the garden also.

FAMILY DYSFUNCTION LEADS TO FEWER HEALTHY RELATIONSHIP SKILLS

Most of this book has been spent describing the way addiction robs families of health. Most of us in families like this don't have basic skills for carrying on healthy relationships; e.g., communication skills, problem-solving skills, parenting skills, negotiating skills, skills for handling conflict.

Some problems may be alleviated as we learn important relationship skills that became lost in our families. First, we need to find out what we don't know. This takes time and help. I didn't know the simplest things, like how to say "I think . . ." or "I feel . . ." rather than "You make me . . ." or "You always think you . . ." I also didn't have a clue about how two people in a marriage worked together for something. I always experienced relationships as one person taking power and the other surrendering power—and I knew which side I wanted to be on!

FEWER RELATIONSHIP SKILLS LEAD TO MORE UNMET NEEDS

Are you aware of your needs? Can you put them into words? How much pain are you in as a result of unmet needs? (Starting to cry when you read the questions is a good tip-off!) We all need love. We need affection. We need attention. We need respect. We need safety. We need time to ourselves. We need to hope and to trust. We need to have integrity. And we need to feel connected to a Higher Power, to others, and to ourselves. An important sign of recovery comes when we stop reacting from our unmet needs and begin to be able to identify our needs and express them in words. This requires skill in relationships. This may also be a trouble spot as we may find out we are in a relationship with someone who is unable, or unwilling, to meet our needs.

UNMET NEEDS LEAD TO MORE ANXIETY AND FRUSTRATION

Some of our anxiety stems from that granddaddy of all diseases—our *dis-ease* at our separateness from God and from each other, or what some refer to as "the human condition." I remember a story about the devil fighting to keep people from God. The devil was convinced he had won because he had the power to distract people with great misery and seduce people with greed and lust for power and possessions.

He laughed at God, saying, "You'll never have these people!"

God said, "You shall *not* have them, for at the core of their being I gave them all a deep longing to know me and the knowledge that they can always come home to me."

My husband believes that this desire, experienced by us all as an emptiness which causes us anxiety, is the motivating force in our lives that moves us toward God and can only be filled through our spiritual life.

Many people have accused the addiction/recovery field of "repackaging" the "human condition" and calling it codependency. Life is difficult enough to navigate for people who come from relatively healthy families—families not so burdened and changed by addictions, illness, and trauma beyond their control. Healthy, functional families can be said to experience the level of anxiety that is natural to experience, given the human condition. When families are dysfunctional, or functioning in pain, the anxiety is immeasurably greater and very real.

We usually don't know we have anxiety. Instead we react to it. The more dysfunctional our situation is, the fewer relationship skills we have to go about getting our most basic needs—as well as our deepest needs—met, and the greater is our anxiety.

Is your level of anxiety so high you are having an impossible time stopping destructive patterns? If this is the case, perhaps you need to focus for now on learning more skills to handle or view your relationships differently in order to calm your anxiety. Working out anxiety and pain with a therapist or in a supportive group may be an important first step.

Some of us are so filled with anxiety and have so little control over how we react in relationships that we can be dangerous to ourselves or to others. If you find yourself in this situation, ask for special help from your therapist.

ANXIETY LEADS TO COMPULSIVE OUTLETS

Our anxiety is the nameless inner agitation we use drugs to, eat to, have sex to, spend to, gamble to, rage to, and caretake to overcome.

What compulsive outlets are you caught up in? Are you feeding your feelings, soothing them with nicotine, caffeine, alcohol, prescription or street drugs? Are you running away through work, exercise, sex, or unhealthy relationships? How can you dare to feel your feelings and see what's there— maybe at first only for a few minutes in group therapy, maybe for an entire evening next week. Then one day you may begin to let go of the ways you run from your pain. Eventually, our goal is to have access to all of our emotions, to know how we feel, to be able to take good care of ourselves, to stop taking care of others, and to live a reasonably healthy, balanced life—free from shame-producing addictions and compulsions.

COMPULSIVE OUTLETS MAKE US VULNERABLE TO ADDICTION

Compulsive outlets are the entrance into the revolving door that keeps addiction going through generations. What is our family legacy of compulsions, addictions, and dysfunction?

How many generations has this been going on, and who will be the one to fight for change?

The supposition is that it takes three generations to recover and develop a heritage of healthy family relationships and to bring our anxiety down to normal proportions. My mom and dad went into recovery when they were forty-six and fifty-five and then were able to see what was happening to their children and help us into recovery. When I went into recovery at twenty-seven I began seeing what was happening to my children. My children began treatment ten years ago, when they were five, seven, and nine years old. We are all still working hard.

ADDICTION CAUSES FAMILY DYSFUNCTION AND ANOTHER GENERATION IS AFFECTED

While we are working on ourselves, we need to stay atuned to our marriage and to our children and their needs and problems. If we are to do our best in this generation to stop the downward spiral of addiction, we must contend with our marriage and help our children after, or often at the *same time*—as we help ourselves.

There is a healthy difference between "writing off" kids or a spouse affected by our family's legacy of addiction and "letting go" when we've done what we can do. I've seen many people who, six months into recovery, will kick a troubled fifteen-year-old out of the house rather than try to get help or treatment for him or her. The same frequently happens with a spouse. It's easy to say, "I have to work on my recovery, and this kid or this relationship is too troubled and too distracting." This is just a perpetuation of chaos, not a healthy solution.

We may have to put our own therapy on a back burner in order to do therapy with or about a spouse or child.

Again, find a strong, family-oriented therapist who also understands addiction.

BOUNDARIES

The concept of boundaries is a particularly important recovery issue. Not understanding and developing clear boundaries keeps us in a position to give and get too much or too little, abuse others or be abused, constantly to second-guess ourselves and exercise poor judgment in personal and professional relationships.

A boundary is a line that marks a limit. Everyone has had the experience of backing away from someone who stands too close. An invisible line demarcates the space around us that we need to feel comfortable; that distance differs for each person and for various situations. Personal boundaries are like a second skin that protects us from harm by warning us when we are being invaded mentally, emotionally, and physically. Hand in hand with well-developed personal boundaries goes a sense of how to handle situations that crowd or threaten these boundaries.

Certain traumas and family relationships destroy or hamper the development of this sense of safety and judgment in relationships. The most tragic and obvious destroyers of that boundary protecting us from harm are incest, rape, sexual abuse, and physical abuse. A more subtle destroyer or inhibitor of boundary development is an enmeshed relationship. Enmeshment commonly happens when parents seek too much emotional support from a child. The parent's need may manifest itself in control (which has a thousand forms); a childlike dependency; cultivating a confidant relationship; a spoken or unspoken alliance with a child that excludes the other parent or other children; or neglect of the child's emotional and physical needs with a parent's needs coming first. These dynamics, by the way, can occur in the best of families who have no control over situations like illness or other tragedies. I can have just as much anger, pain, and regret about what happened to my family during my father's five-year bout with cancer as another person might feel because of her mother's alcoholism or sex addiction.

Personal boundaries are like common sense: you either have it or you don't. There's no such thing as having a little bit of common sense. Anyone who has developed judgment late in life knows what a slow and exhausting process it is.

Discovering and developing personal boundaries when they were unclear or nonexistent is equally slow and exhausting. We learn we can apply values in our dealings with people; we can say no if a man (or woman) at an AA meeting tries to coerce or manipulate us into doing something we don't want or intended not to do. We learn we do not have to stay in an uncomfortable situation, that we have a right to get up and leave. We learn to distinguish between discomfort in a situation that's good for us (an intense therapy session) and one that hurts us (a family fight that could lead to violence). We stay for the therapy session (unless something is wrong) and leave the family fight with a promise to continue after things settle down. We learn to apply values and ethics to everyday situations; no matter how badly we want to believe that we can go into business with a dynamic man we know from our AA meetings who says he will make us a million dollars, we decline because we know he is gambling compulsively and his ideas are unethical.

Carl Sandburg once said that certain words "wear long boots, hard boots." Learning the power of words, then finding out when to use them and with whom, is another critical area of growth in establishing stronger, clearer boundaries. I remember talking with my children's therapist when I had been sober two years. During my second or third visit, she said something that made me laugh and feel equal and accepted. I said to her, "Maxine, I love you!" All she said was, "Huh, you love me?" Although I anguished over that interaction for days, somehow I hadn't felt diminished by it and added it to my knowledge about boundaries. I exercise much more judgment about who, where, and in what context I use powerful words like "love" and gestures like hugs.

When I taught adolescent girls to say "I like you," rather than "I love you," to attractive boys, they became aware of a stage in a boyfriend-girlfriend relationship. "I like you" implies and gives permission for a friendship stage in these relationships, while they understood "I love you" to imply immediate commitment and sex.

Words are magic wands. A few new words and phrases can generate a feeling of real inner power. It may even feel a little scary, but you will begin to see that you can influence your own life and give it new direction. Try using a few of the following phrases and see whether they make a real change in your life:

> *"I'm not sure what I think or feel—give me a minute."*
>
> *"I choose to . . ."*
>
> *"What I need from you is . . ."*
>
> *"I prefer not to do that."*
>
> *"I need time alone right now."*
>
> *"I don't like . . ."*
>
> *"This is the situation (what you are upset about). These are my feelings (hurt, scared, mad, etc.). This is what I need (I just need you to listen, I need your help, I need to be held, etc.)."*

We have countless other such words and phrases in our language. They need not be spoken angrily or defiantly, although they usually are at first. Clear, direct messages draw clear, direct boundaries. These boundaries allow not only a feeling of security, but also a sense of self-respect and dignity.

Possessing boundaries is like owning a computer that automatically solves complicated problems for us and presents us with the answers we need. Lacking boundaries is like handling these complex problems with a pad and paper before we know how to read or write.

Establishing personal boundaries may begin with saying to someone for the first time, "No, I don't feel mad, I think I feel hurt." "Mind-reading" is a subtle destroyer of boundaries. Many parents fall into the trap of telling their children what they should feel or what they do feel. Have you ever been furious or overwhelmed when you realized someone was telling you what you thought or felt? It is even worse to become strong enough to challenge such an intrusion by saying what you REALLY feel and see your own interpretation rejected. What an assault upon a new, fragile boundary! A person might think, "Gee, maybe I don't know how I feel after all. Maybe I am crazy. On the other hand, maybe I am so sick of people telling me how I feel and what I think that I can't be open." It helps to check out these situations with a therapist, group, sponsor, or healthy friend who can say, "No, you're not crazy. Who knows your feelings better than you?" After a time we know ourselves well enough to trust our healthy reactions and take stronger stands when we need to detach and leave an unhealthy power struggle without losing our selves.

Boundaries also grow with the realization, "I don't know this person well enough to hug her and I'm not comfortable hugging people I don't know." Hugging, by the way, is one of the greatest saboteurs of boundary development. A friend and I were discussing boundary issues in treatment programs and the potential pitfalls for patients. She gave a perfect example when she said, "In our (outpatient) group last night we spent the entire time on boundaries. When group was over, we closed, and I said, 'Okay. Everybody give and get hugs.'"

When this issue comes up in a group, some people admit that they have unwillingly tolerated being touched when they didn't want to be simply because they were told to, and they didn't dare risk expressing their feelings. The concept of boundaries is an important new insight in the treatment of addictions.

FAMILY BOUNDARIES

Families with boundary problems practice "group think"; they think and feel collectively as a group, and individual differences provoke anxiety. You need to be prepared for your family to feel anxiety when you try to change. In the long run, family members who need recovery will join you one by one as they become less frightened and their need becomes greater.

Early in my education about family systems, I heard the remark, "Individuality is searched out and beaten down." If Mom is angry at Aunt Sally, the whole family has to be angry with her too or get involved in patching up the relationship. Or if you begin going to Twelve Step meetings and therapy, relatives may feel threatened to the point of subtly or blatantly sabotaging your involvement. It might be as innocent as a husband "forgetting" he was supposed to watch the kids while you go to your meeting. It may be as blatant as derision or even fights when you try to leave.

Enmeshed families also practice group emotions. When one person starts to cry about a personal hurt, everybody else joins in the tears. Asked, "Why?", they invariably respond, "It hurts to see him hurt." When one person is in a bad mood, the whole family participates or feels subdued or "jumps through hoops" to bring him out of his funk "so we can all be happy." Whole families also act out an emotion, such as anger, that really belongs to only one person who won't express it or is unaware of it. Harriet Lerner writes well about this topic in her book, *The Dance of Anger:* A child becomes ill every time the parents fight, with the unconscious goal to bring the parents together in their concern about the child. A man feels passively furious at his wife, and their child physically abuses her mother. Mom is angry at one child, and the whole family punishes him with abuse or isolation.

These enmeshed families cannot tolerate one member's deviation from the group's collective viewpoint. If Dad believes "the Union is the only way to go and management stinks," an adult son cannot disagree without a fight. In a conflict between two sisters, everybody else has to choose sides. If a powerful family member is angry, the others must feel angry too or risk "choosing the other side" and being abused. A less powerful member must surrender anger or be made miserable. Weak members may try to keep thoughts and feelings secret, but the others invariably find them out.

Each person has a unique way of looking at the world, and these differences enrich everybody's life. In enmeshed families, a difference of opinion is a personal statement that the others are wrong. They must either change the deviant's thinking, or come to a new consensus in order to settle the anxiety. Enmeshed families tend to operate at two extremes. One is in a constant state of chaos, endlessly examining and changing their collective mind. Another rigidly holds on to ideas and opinions that are not helpful to individual members. The first family is so burdened by limitless options that its members are constantly frustrated, venting their frustration on each other and society. The other causes children to learn early to censor what they see outside the family in order to cope with an unrealistic system, in which change is too threatening.

People can try, but no one has a right to tell you what to think and feel. Maybe you've lived this way for a long time. There is nothing more important to take a stand about than your right to get help and find recovery. Therapy needs to be as family-oriented as possible. If it's not possible to involve your family in therapy, your therapist and group can help you change the destructive patterns you become aware of.

PERSONAL BELONGINGS AND PERSONAL SPACES

People whose personal possessions have never been treated with respect will understand the importance of this boundary issue. Surviving a troubled family may require a little space and time we consider to be our own. If we can't count on people knocking before they open our door or asking before they use our things, we feel vulnerable and anxious about the one area of our life we might have been able to control.

A particular problem in chaotic families is that many children get into trouble with each other sexually. Sometimes unhealthy sexual experiences occur because there is no privacy. Parents may not have the awareness or parenting skills to help kids make transitions in their relationships. A brother and sister take baths together when they are small, for example, sleep with each other for the fun of it, pinch each other on the bottom or chest, wrestle, change clothes in one another's presence, barge into the bathroom or bedrooms whenever they like, and so on. Understanding parents can help kids change and set limits appropriate for their ages and their relationships.

When destructive sexual acting out has occurred, we need immediate help to assess the damage and find a healthy direction. A family-oriented therapist helps open up these critical issues between us and our children. Parents need to begin therapy with children, by the way. We would only reinforce destructive patterns and shame if we were to "drop the kids off to be fixed" in a one-to-one relationship with a therapist or go to therapy by ourselves, leaving the children out, because we are too scared to find out what damage we have done.

For long-term change in this area, we need a framework for living our lives. Learning how to respect others and insist that others respect us is the real work of boundary setting. These guidelines and activities may help.

▶ Find a Twelve Step program. The Twelve Steps offer a healthy framework for living.
▶ Find a healthy therapist who understands boundary-setting and generational family issues.
▶ Don't read minds. Share your thoughts and feelings and ask what the other person thinks or feels and then let it be.
▶ Teach everyone in your home about privacy. Find out where and when people like to be alone and respect it.

- Pick a topic at a meal or during a car ride and find out what each person feels and thinks on this issue.
- Each person who wants to participate can pick a feeling to look for and recognize in herself this day. Talk about it at the end of the day.
- Make agreements about what personal belongings we are willing to share and what is private property. Knocking on doors and asking permission is a must.
- Learn to say "I think" when expressing a thought and "I feel" when expressing a feeling. Keep working at it until it becomes a new habit.
- Find a good parenting program to learn important skills and to find support.

THE BOUNDARIES OF OUR CONSCIENCE

The concept of conscience clarifies each family member's adaptation to the glaring discrepancies stemming from the addiction. Losing conscience, the ability to recognize the difference between right and wrong, and losing the ability to live according to good values must be understood and incorporated into recovery. To say "whose values are you using to set the standard?" only clouds the issue and perpetuates the problem. Hundreds of families have diagnosed conscience with me; few people have not agreed that we all share basic human values such as honesty, treating others and ourselves with respect and kindness, working hard to be "good" people and to contribute to life in spiritual ways.

Imagine conscience being defined by a boundary line, just as the property around our home is marked by a fence or a room is defined by its walls. If all the behavior inside the boundary is "right" behavior and all the behavior outside the boundary is "wrong" behavior, what keeps us inside the boundary? People answer this question in a variety of ways: my conscience keeps me inside the line; my values; fear of consequences; morals; good upbringing; my parents; my spouse; society's norms; God's laws; I might get in trouble; ethical standards; what other people might think.

Some of the forces are internal (values, morals, conscience, ethics), and some are external forces (fear of consequences, parents, spouse, societal norms, what others might think). Most addicts have not developed the internal muscle, as my husband calls it, to cope with life on a day-to-day basis, but rely instead on external forces to keep their behavior in line.

This way of life stems from addicts' core of shame and the belief that they are basically bad, unworthy people and that no one would love them as they are. Hiding from those beliefs results in "pseudo-beliefs," ideals they would like to live by, but the behavior they repeat over and over betrays the core of shame and the beliefs forged by addiction.

Some family members of addicts have a strongly developed sense of right and wrong and dysfunction that shows up in other areas. They cannot fathom someone who does not do right. A parent, for example, who is humiliated into paying off his child's bad checks believes this will be the event which will get through to his child and cause him to change. And of course, the child plays along by displaying remorse which may be real or a deliberate manipulation, depending on the child.

Therapists in the addiction field have always said that addicts stop developing emotionally when they start using a chemical. A twenty-six-year-old, a fifty-year-old and an eighteen-year-old could all be fourteen years old emotionally, if all three started using at that age. There is the obvious emotional component, and there is also the behavioral component. If a teenager's beloved grandmother dies and he goes to the funeral loaded on pot, he eventually has to deal with his pain about his loss but he also has to process his shame about not seeing her during the last months of her life and going loaded to her funeral.

When an addict stops practicing an addiction, all his energy must go into dealing with the most immediate problems, like getting through an indecent-exposure arrest and finding a new job. The longer he is committed to recovery, the deeper he works into the issues and emotions he did not pick up through a natural process of maturity.

As for the behavioral component of development, an addict doesn't go through the necessary transition from living his parents' values, assuming that they provided a good model, to making those values his own. Healthy beliefs about self lead to healthy values; they are the boundary of conscience.

Until early adolescence, most people control their behavior with their parents' values (the ones parents practice, not the ones they preach) and by relying on the external control they supply. A child doesn't take a cookie because Mom said not to, and he might get into trouble. The children of non-smoking parents are more likely not to smoke cigarettes than the children of smokers. If parents practice good values, adolescents begin to adopt them as their own.

The world puts these values to the test. A girl whose companions are shoplifting must decide on the spot whether to value honesty or acceptance. If the only reason she doesn't participate is a fear of getting caught (external force), she will have to decide for herself sooner or later. If her friends continue to steal and don't get caught, she might join them eventually. She is also in a quandary if she opts for honesty and tries to carry on relationships with dishonest friends.

A normal human being who crosses the boundary and violates conscience by doing something wrong feels guilty, scared of consequences, remorseful, mad at herself, ashamed, or embarrassed, depending on her own character and the nature of the wrong. To make these uncomfortable feelings go away, she can either get back inside the boundary by righting the wrong or change the boundary, thus making the wrong act right. She accomplishes this moral contortion by rationalizing, defending, blaming, or justifying.

Changing the boundary of conscience in this way begins the path toward spiritual death. The further she strays from living right, the more shame she experiences unaware, and the more sophisticated her mental defenses become. She begins to restrict the people she can spend time with. She by-passes shame and emotions and runs instead to intellect for justification to continue living as she is. Fairly quickly, she loses touch with conscience.

All addicts experience this process of erosion, unaware that their addiction is pulling them away from their values. Instead, they rationalize the loss, believing that family and circumstances are pushing them away. A sex addict does not know, for example, that his sex addiction is requiring him to go cruising for a prostitute. Instead he picks a fight with his wife and tells himself that, if she weren't such a cold bitch, he wouldn't need to go elsewhere. He leaves her behind, wondering in her heart what defect in her makes her husband stray. She knows where her husband is going, which only deepens her shame, fear, and confusion. She confides in her daughter, who overheard the fight, and her daughter is beside herself because she's heard her father on the phone with other women.

This wife violates her own values by confiding in her daughter, lying to her mother later that evening, apologizing to her husband to keep the peace when he comes home later, reeking of cheap perfume, and having sex with him despite her knowledge that she isn't the only woman he has em-braced tonight.

The daughter crosses the boundary of her conscience by not telling her mother what she knows, by acting nice to her father while she hates his guts, and by losing her temper and telling her brother all about what Dad is doing, even though she promised Mom she wouldn't tell a soul.

Brother storms out of the house, finds a kid from school who has marijuana, and gets loaded, which used to be out-side the boundary of his conscience, telling himself life sucks, so why not get loaded?

Little sister only knows that everyone is upset and hurting and wonders how to make them feel better.

This process devastates the family as an environment. Since most sex addicts grew up in very dysfunctional fami-lies, they usually have been in the process of losing touch with their conscience and emotions since childhood, often having experienced childhood sexual trauma and begun to act out early. Many spouses of sex addicts also grew up in sexually dysfunctional families, in alcoholism, or in rigid fundamentalist religious families. What happens to the family members of this sex addict while he is losing any last shred of conscience to his addiction? They go right along with him. Mom reacts to Dad's loss of conscience by becoming more and more restricted in her sense of right and wrong. As the addiction worsens, she takes on more and more responsibility in order to keep peace and to cope. Perhaps one or two of their children reacting in the same way, while another uses alcohol and drugs.

Children of sex addicts lose the simple concept of right and wrong behavior. They are only guilty, ashamed, and depressed, or grandiose and self-righteous, assigning blame and responsibility for their behavior to anyone and anything outside of themselves. The more generations of dysfunction, the worse the loss for everyone.

The effect of changing boundaries is extreme because most people have a desire or need to be "good people" and to be perceived as "good" by the world around them. It is through living beliefs that people feel a continuous sense of worth and self-esteem. They say to themselves, "I am a good person and I validate that through my behavior."

A person with an intact sense of worth undergoes considerable stress as he begins to make room for behavior that breaches his beliefs or conscience. My husband says he'll never forget the first time he decided to do something wrong. While visiting a friend of the family who happened to be handicapped, he crept into her room, stole a penny from her purse and ran as fast as his five-year-old legs would carry him to the nearest store. He bought the biggest piece of gum he could see and jumped outside to have one of the most nerve-wracking chews of his life. In mid-chew, he saw a man coming down the street toward him and knew with dread and certainty that the man knew about the heinous crime and had come to deliver the punishment Rick knew he deserved. He tore the gum out of his mouth, threw the damning evidence down a grill and raced back to his mother and her friend, never to commit another such act for many years to come.

I myself remember going to confession with my schoolmates when we were ten years old. For the first time I had committed a crime I was scared to confess. My misdeed was probably similar to Rick's theft of the penny, except I think I would have enjoyed the gum, thought up a lie to tell if I got caught, and gone back the next day for another penny or stolen the gum from the store. Anyway, as I knelt in the church, reflecting on my sins, I could only think about how to avoid telling the sin that might get me into trouble. I knew I had to confess all my sins for the obvious Catholic reasons, like going to purgatory. In those days, children confessed by counting their offenses: "I told three lies, I hit my brother twice, and I disobeyed my parents four times." After considerable pondering, I found the answer! I would omit the troublesome sin from my confession and tack another one on to the "lie section" of my list!

All of us remember such incidents in our lives. We sometimes wander outside our conscience and experience the guilt and discomfort of such behavior. If we are lucky, we are able to pull ourselves back inside the boundary and restore ourselves to a sense of well-being. Obviously, not everyone leads such a simple or fortunate life. Some lose control over their lives and cannot return to healthy behavior. Others, like the Catholic girl, never had a stable or well-developed source of values from the beginning. That lack does not in the least diminish their desire to be "good" people, but it does make their lives more confusing and difficult.

Put simply, as people expand the boundary of their conscience, their self-worth diminishes. To make matters worse, as self-worth lessens, they grasp for something to soothe their pain. Tragically, they often reach for the thing that started the problem in the first place, and the cycle of self-destruction begins again.

It isn't simple or easy to change behavior and to re-develop, or develop for the first time, a healthy sense of right and wrong.

Many family members of addicts ask the question in treatment, "Why does she lie all the time? She lies even when it would be easier to tell the truth!" The answer is simple. She's been lying so long she lost her conscience about lying long ago.

A thirty-year-old man in treatment felt horribly ashamed about the events leading up to his treatment. He came home drunk one night and raped his wife when she refused to have sex with him. During a fight the next day, she asked him to leave. One of his sons got scared and grabbed him around the leg. The man had struck his son and knocked him across the room. He wondered why he was so ashamed about these incidents but had no conscience about lying. It made sense to him that he would feel ashamed about breaking down a new boundary in his conscience. He had never raped his wife or anyone else, and he had never hit his kids before, but lying was old hat. It had been seventeen years since he had felt guilty about lying to his parents, and twelve years earlier, he had started lying to his wife.

The man wanted to know how to regain his conscience about lying. I thought for a minute and told him to tell the truth for six months. He laughed at me and said, "It's harder than that, isn't it?" I laughed at him because I knew how hard it would be!

For the first three months of recovery, the young man probably catches himself a few, or many, times before he tells a lie. Then he trips up, and a lie sometimes slips out. Sometimes he recognizes the lapse soon after it happens, admits it, and sets it right. This effort is incredibly difficult, depending on the circumstances, and he might need the help of his therapy group and Twelve Step program sponsor to stay rigorously honest.

In the fourth month of his commitment, in a family therapy group, his mom talks about her caretaking behavior; she thought it was her job to make her son get up every morning. Everyone laughs except her son and his wife. We find out that his wife took over that job, which is a real problem because she can't get him out of bed, and he gets mad if she doesn't try. This blind spot triggers the young man's shame when it comes out in group, but he works through his embarrassment and grudgingly decides to change this behavior. About a week later he forgets to set his alarm and arrives at work late. He has a last-chance contract with his boss, so out of fear, he lies. He says he had a flat tire on the freeway and didn't have a spare.

If this young man is "working a program of recovery" he does something healthy now, like call his sponsor, who knows all about his commitment to tell the truth. His sponsor will tell him to get to a Twelve Step meeting during his lunch hour. His group is discussing the Tenth Step: "We continued to take personal inventory and, when we were wrong, promptly admitted it."

He knows what he needs to do. He may call a member of his therapy group for support first, but then he tells his boss the truth. Now, because God tends to wrap his arms around newly recovering people, one of two things happens. Perhaps his boss is so impressed that he says wonderful things to him and takes him off his last-chance contract.

Perhaps his boss fires him, in which case he goes right over to see a friend who is in his Twelve Step group and stays there until the next meeting. He's scared to death, angry with himself for lying, but proud for telling the truth, and sad about the prospect of telling his wife that he lost his job. Because God takes special care of people new in recovery, he is called on for the first time to share in the meeting. He tells what has happened and expresses gratitude that he is here rather than doing something destructive. An old guy with twenty years of recovery approaches him after the meeting, slaps him on the back and says, "I'm putting a crew together. Why not come around tomorrow and put in an application?"

Two more months go by, and the young man finds that his hard work has built a conscience about telling the truth. Now the boundary separating right from wrong about lying is clearly defined and strong. If he crosses the line, he experiences guilt. He may test himself once in a while, but the guilt eats at him and affects other areas of his life if he doesn't right his wrong; in Twelve Step programs, we say, "We have to be rigorously honest" to keep our recovery. He will also need continually to challenge himself to develop his conscience about other behaviors and attitudes as they present themselves. Anyone who is unable to change a behavior needs to explore that problem with a therapist and a group and consider what the obstacle could be. Shame keeps people lying, for example, as does an addiction.

SECRETS

Addicts and families who are beginning recovery fear the disclosure of secrets. The kinds of secrets vary, but the fears are similar: "What will happen if they know?" "Everyone will hate me." "We will be torn apart." Keeping secrets in therapy eventually becomes a major factor in unhappy relationships and relapse.

Considering the amount of stress that dysfunctional families experience, their attempts to avoid any further pain in their lives are no surprise. They have little experience in true resolution of problems. There is only the endless cycle of good intentions and failed attempts to change. So when faced with the decision to expose the most painful and traumatic issues in their lives, families understandably don't view this occasion as an opportunity for healing.

What people cannot see is that the damage has already been done. Yes, it is possible to cause more problems by these revelations, but that is why we so strongly recommend the help of experienced professionals. We believe secrets need to come out for the sake of the person carrying the secret and for the sake of the family.

My husband's most unusual lesson about secrets came from a veterinarian. His pet cockatiel accidentally caught his leg in the refrigerator door and broke it. We didn't notice right away because he acted as if nothing were wrong, he continued eating, preening, and playing as though he were completely normal. Many creatures, the vet explained, learn to keep secrets. It's a natural act of survival.

It seems that injured birds attract unwanted attention from predators, so if a flock senses a "defective" bird, they drive the bird out. Even with an injury as serious as a broken leg, the bird acts as though nothing were wrong. The penalty for revealing the secret would be total rejection by his own kind.

Had we not noticed the injury, the leg would have worsened. The bird could have died from infection or the leg would have partially healed, leaving him with a crippled and ineffective leg. As bad as the initial trauma was, even greater damage would have resulted.

This example of animal behavior illuminates some important aspects of human secrecy. The word "denial" is used to describe the manner of secretive people, but when confronted with this concept, many feel they are being accused of intentionally hiding information. Denial by itself does not adequately explain the difficulty people have in revealing their secrets. Keeping secrets about painful and embarrassing situations is natural and normal. It is natural in the sense that avoiding pain seems to be an automatic response. It is normal in the sense that most people seem to respond in a similar fashion. Although keeping secrets may not be the most healthy response, most people do it. A friend of mine used to say that a recovering alcoholic is abnormal; recovery is an "unnatural" state for an alcoholic to be in. It may be some comfort to know that having a lot of problems may be quite normal for a situation. Secrecy about trauma or pain is sometimes a natural survival tactic. That is nothing to feel guilty about. While teaching the values of honesty and truthfulness, families also warn children not to talk about family matters; after all, "what will people think?" The implication is that something terrible may happen to the abuser, and the child will have to bear the additional burden of guilt if that happens. Or perhaps others won't love and approve of him, making the world a very unsafe place. In families that have secrets, you can talk about ANYTHING, just as long as you don't talk about EVERYTHING.

Secrets aren't necessarily hidden information, but are often common knowledge so bound by shame, they are not to be discussed. In a family where Mom is a compulsive over-eater, everyone sees her in the kitchen standing by the cup-board eating one sandwich after another. But nobody is allowed to talk about it. When I weighed 220 pounds, my biggest secret was that I was fat. Not knowing their own thoughts, feelings, and beliefs makes people feel safer from rejection. In generational dysfunction, the family rule "don't talk" is an endlessly repeated lesson that becomes natural and ordinary. It is the normalization of dysfunction.

Sexual traumas have a particular kind of power over our lives. Children who experience trauma are usually young and relatively powerless. The abusers are usually people who seem to have almost total control over the children's lives. And because every abuser needs to have a victim, he cannot teach the child about the power of choices and independent decisions. Since children who suffer incest are taught to be victims, they are commonly abused throughout their lives by a variety of people.

Dysfunctional families have a way of holding back love and acceptance as a means of discipline and control. Adult children from these families are lucky if they can make changes that allow for loving and warm relationships despite past secrets. There are many whose relationships do not improve significantly or take many years to stabilize. Many others who are fortunate to find a few loving, warm, and safe relationships end up projecting the childhood trauma into their work, parenting, or physical health.

It isn't only the initial abuse that does the damage; the fear-kept secret also destroys. Tremendous damage comes from the constant cycling of guilt and shame. Repeated patterns set up around diseased behavior become ingrained, even in recoveries. Revealing secrets may seem to burden the "betrayer" with further responsibility, and may also cause rejection by his own. So families keep the secrets, believing themselves to be the unlovely, the unworthy few. Like that poor old bird and his secret injury, shame makes a wound that never heals or that mends crookedly and cripples the family.

A secret has three phases: its ORIGIN in what happened; the REACTION in an unconscious reflex of feelings and behavior; and the RESPONSE, a conscious decision about the way to deal with the secret. RESPONSE implies action based upon a conscious decision to confront a part of the past. Many people never reach the third phase. Relatively few people intentionally seek help unless they are forced to it by interventions, crisis, and sheer luck. But the readers of this book are standing at the road of opportunity, able to take control of their lives by the power to decide.

Revealing a secret is never easy and should never be taken lightly. Some secrets are extremely painful and even dangerous. Keeping the lid clamped down can cause a great pressure to build inside, like the steam in a car radiator that has overheated. It's safer to allow the steam to escape a little at a time because removing the cap can cause an explosion of water and steam. The discussion of family secrets can cause great anxiety, fearfulness, nightmares, and other difficulties. That fact is the reason that trained counselors are so important to recovery.

The fear of revealing a secret is usually worse than the secret itself. Families convince themselves that the worst will happen if people know. I once had a patient who announced in a private session that he had a terrible secret to share, but he couldn't do so yet because it was too horrible to face the group's reaction. Two days later, he haltingly choked out the terrifying story: he was gay. The group members, expecting stories of murder, torture, or whatever their imaginations had manufactured, looked at one another as if to say, "but what's the secret?" Now that he had overcome this initial hurdle, I think my friend was a little disappointed to hear so little reaction. As he said later, what's the sense of scaring yourself half to death if no one's going to appreciate it?

Some secrets are relatively easy to deal with. Although it may be embarrassing to admit such things as compulsive spending or lying to a spouse, secrets like these can usually be dealt with simply and directly. Sexual abuse or affairs can be another matter. Secrets such as these should never be revealed without help. In some cases, part of secret-telling is sharing the information with significant others like family members and even confronting people who abused us. If it is to be done at all, it is vital that these painful and traumatic revelations *always* be planned with the guidance of a trained, experienced helper. What you reveal probably is less important than *when* you reveal it, and assistance of a professional therapist in such decisions can be invaluable. The most important thing is that the secret be told to SOMEONE, and that people resume the power over their own lives.

People sometimes hesitate to reveal secrets because of the damage the revelation may do others, but they fail to see that the damage has already been done. The denial and delusion of their disease lead them to think that they have successfully hidden their painful past. In family therapy sessions relatives are rarely surprised that something was going on. Needless to say, what people really fear is the reaction the others will have toward them.

That's the great thing about groups—sometimes the acceptance is more overwhelming than the secrets. Often other people have kept similar or even "worse" secrets. The beauty is that it's a safe place with people like us. Many adult children came from families where feeling safe was as unlikely as feeling sane. Trusting other people may be difficult at first because it's such a new experience, but in a Twelve Step group, experienced people can guide newcomers. Their caring can speed healing and make the difference between merely surviving life and living life fully.

People who are busy ducking pain cannot focus their hearts and minds on the healing power that surrounds them. A loving and growing relationship with God and other people requires ever-increasing trust, vulnerability, and commitment. Getting well is hard work, but people do recover. That old cockatiel healed up just fine, but he avoids refrigerators as if they all had cats inside, and that isn't so bad. Because of his injury, he has learned some things that left him better off than he was before. Don't let secrets keep you from the life you deserve.

Chapter Ten

Stages of Recovery

I t is a truism that recovery is a journey and not a destination. This chapter, based on Dr. Timmen Cermak's book, *Diagnosing and Treating Co-Dependence*, will not describe the whole trip, but just the occasional places of interest.

Many people go through three stages of recovery, with emphasis on a different task in each stage:

1. Victimization and education
2. Survival and action
3. Transformation and reunion

These stages and tasks represent a changing attitude toward self. This summary of a common pattern makes recovery sound simple and neat, but of course each individual recovers in his own way. The stages overlap one another, and some people even find themselves shifting back and forth between stages. Such fluctuations are perfectly normal and even necessary at times.

VICTIMIZATION AND EDUCATION

People in recovery sometimes feel that they are blaming others when they begin to discuss the addictions and dysfunction in their lives. We adult children have always covered up for others and felt guilty for everything that happened to us. We are not ducking responsibility, but learning to distinguish our own from others' dysfunction.

It is important to give up two beliefs, first the idea that you are capable of handling everything by yourself, and then the further misconception that you are responsible for everything that happened to you. These beliefs result from a lifetime of training. Feeling capable of handling everything alone comes from learning that people cannot be trusted, especially important people in your life. This distrust does not imply a lack of love or caring for those people, but merely that something important may be missing in the relationship.

The origin could be something simple like inconsistent parenting or something more obvious like an act of incest. When we unconsciously see that parents are not always consistent or trustworthy, we instinctively try to create security by controlling our own lives. Finding someone else who gives us that feeling often leads to harmful, dependent relationships.

At the same time, we develop the belief that these important people are acting inconsistently because of something we have done. The obvious action for any child is to keep changing his "faulty behavior." No wonder these beliefs make people feel a little crazy. We try to please and help people by changing our behavior in the hope we will get what we need from them. At the same time we shut everybody out by trying to control everything around us.

Involvement in therapy or a support group is an educational process. Education allows detachment and gradually increasing commitment to the recovery process. Members of a group learn that others have undergone the same experience. Some feel nothing at all as they begin to examine their lives, while others may begin to feel quite anxious. A group or sponsor helps a newcomer to travel at a safe speed.

As we learn more about recovery, we learn that we developed a pattern of interaction in our families in order to survive, and we have brought those behaviors with us to adulthood. They have served us well, perhaps not made us happy, but they have gotten us through. Besides, our pattern is all we know. That's why we must be a part of therapy— it is education, the least threatening of all means to begin recovery.

In our early recovery, we label ourselves adult children of sex addicts. We talk of victimization, of events beyond our control or ability to understand. We learn that we have adopted an unrealistic and diseased sense of shame and guilt, blaming ourselves for things we did not do. We accept the label of victim because it helps us understand and gives us clarity to the past. Unfortunately, we cannot continue generalizing; we must begin to talk in detail about people, places, and things in order to understand specifically what happened. You may have remembered and recorded many important events while reading through the charted characteristics. Sharing these memories with a group and a therapist will give you comfort and insight.

We can eventually begin to work with our former responses and feelings. We become involved once again with our inner selves, but with the feeling and belief that we can begin to exert some power and influence over our own lives. We start believing that our life experience will not overwhelm us. We are successful for the first time, for example, in our commitment to stay out of a relationship, and we notice growth as a result.

SURVIVAL AND ACTION

As our recovery continues, we begin to learn about "patterns of interaction," or "survival traits." Many people fail to see that everyone grows up with a limited number of options in life. Abraham H. Maslow once said that if the only tool you have is a hammer, you tend to see every problem as a nail. We go about our lives doing the same thing over and over and expecting different results. We begin to see in this stage of recovery that, although we have only a hammer, it is possible to get different tools.

The one thing worse than having only a hammer is growing up with the belief that you are a nail. It's very difficult to enter into the recovery process when you are afraid that a hammer is waiting for you every time you stick your head up. In this stage, people learn that they can be something other than a nail, but first we must find out how these behaviors met our family's needs and how we used them to survive and meet our own needs.

Recovery is learning that choices exist. In childhood we discovered that believing and acting in certain ways enabled us, however unsatisfactorily, to survive and fulfill our needs. Part of the disease is not really recognizing our dissatisfaction, how deep it goes, and what causes it. We know only unconsciously that certain behaviors "work," so we bring them with us into adulthood. The longer we stay in recovery, the more we see how deep these patterns go, how intertwined they are in our every interaction. They meet needs. They work. It's as though the disease itself were alive, influencing what we want in life. Then we begin to realize just how tough recovery can be. In many ways, it was easier to be sick. It took no effort, no thought, just a surrender to a life that seemed cruel and unfair.

Our discussions about the disease at this point are no longer detached, but begin to take on deep feeling and meaning. There may be anger toward people, a sense of betrayal, deep sadness and feelings of loss. Grief for a lost childhood is predictable, and those with extremely traumatic childhood experiences may regain forgotten memories.

People entering this stage also become painfully aware of compulsive behaviors in their life. When these feelings and memories come roaring up, the anxiety and stress kick-starts compulsions like an old Harley, threatening to take you on the ride of your life. The importance of professional group therapy for help and support cannot be overemphasized.

People in this stage need a safety net as they begin to act. In order to discover your feelings about a person important in your life, for instance, or to practice expressing feelings toward someone, you might write a candid letter to him. Knowing you are not going to send the letter, you are free to say everything you need to say without fear that you might cause harm. In working through this exercise with others, feelings eventually decrease in intensity and the day may come when you can talk face to face.

TRANSFORMATION AND REUNION

Our past traumas are not excuses for the way we are, nor do they keep us prisoner; they are only part of the forces that helped shape us. We now consciously seek new experiences that will shape us in new ways. We give our own lives meaning and direction through a clearer sense of judgment and improved decision-making skills.

Learning about our patterns of interaction suggests that we can change our lives, that we can give them new form and meaning by applying new thoughts, feelings, and behaviors. Trying to fight old patterns can be tiring and exhausting, but each success empowers us a bit more. Each new victory supplies a little more energy and desire. In time, recovery no longer feels like an uphill battle. We are like a runner who has slowly worked himself into good condition. He runs at his own speed, filled with confidence and control, understanding that, as he runs, he is challenging his limitations and enjoying his abilities.

Finally, when we begin to exercise this healthy control and influence, we awaken spiritually to the fundamental awareness necessary for surrender. If we desire a full return to humanity as children of God, there must be no one left to blame. We are responsible from this point on.

Yes, we can still be victimized. Our houses can be robbed, a drunk driver can hit us, we can be overpowered and raped, and many other uncontrollable, unforeseen things can happen. But we learn how to protect ourselves, we minimize possible problems, we find that "luck" owes in part to our decisions, judgment, and hard work.

As we shed some of the anger and rage about the past, we can see more freely the disease that blighted the lives of the people we were blaming. One generation spun its members in chaotic rhythms, setting the next generation in motion. On and on it went, a dance of spiritual death, a dance we decline to join.

Chapter Eleven

From a Lifetime of Beginnings...to the Beginning of a Lifetime

I heard an artist quoted on television: "To draw, we must close our eyes and sing!" I imagined everything inside of me that was honest, all of the music, laughter, and tears flowing to the surface and out to the world, uninhibited by shame and fear. I laughed as I closed my eyes and drew my song. My husband and I always had a joke about not attending any workshop that was advertised with the words, "wear loose clothing." I was always so frightened that I would be asked to do something uncomfortable and not be able to say I didn't want to do it.

Recovery is about risking. From the time we are tiny, when our lives are out of control, control becomes all important. When control becomes so important, the child within us becomes stifled in order to survive. We can only wait for the time in our lives when we're faced with the decision to surrender to the experience of recovery. This is the time we will be reunited with the child we left behind—maybe didn't even know existed.

Within everyone is a flicker of hope waiting to become a flame. This spark of life can be fed by any number of circumstances in our life, but it can also be smothered by fear. The greatest hurdle for me in my recovery came when I had to surrender the person I had been without knowing who I would be on the other side. I had to surrender before having the gifts of faith and trust. I was so frightened, not knowing where life was taking me. Some time later, my mother gave me a wonderful meditation book that described how I felt in letting go of the only life I knew. My husband and I want to share part of it with you.

YOU'RE NOT GOING TO DIE

Her six-year-old son decided to take her into his full confidence. "Mom, when you turn out the lights and it gets dark in here, I'm afraid to die." He watched carefully to see what she would say.

She did not act surprised. She waited a minute, trying to get her bearings, searching for the way to say it. "Dan," she began finally, "before Judy was born, she was warm and comfortable and well-fed, wasn't she? And I can imagine she might have felt, even though she couldn't talk, 'I don't ever want to leave this. I don't want to die.' "

Dan interrupted, "But it isn't the same. Judy wasn't going to die. She was going to be born."

"Exactly," she said. "Only Judy didn't know what it would be like, so let's say she was afraid and called it dying instead. After she was born, though, she discovered that warmth went on, and food, and being wanted and loved."

Dan was listening intently. She continued. "Someday, when Judy gets a little older, she may feel just like you do now—'I don't ever want to leave this place, earth, I don't want to die.' Only something says to her, 'Why, you're not going to die when you leave here. You're going to be born—born into something even greater, even more wonderful, where love and growth and being wanted still go on.' "

Neither of them said anything for a long time.

"We don't know, Dan—none of us knows exactly—and that's the reason we are afraid. But I have a feeling we need not be afraid. That dying is something like being born."

Meditation by Jean Beavin Abernathy from *Meditation for Women*, edited by Jean Beavin Abernathy, Abingdon Press. Copyrighted material reprinted with permission.

Even though many of us were not warm, safe, and well-fed as children, many of us took comfort in knowing what to expect. This book may ask you to believe and maybe surrender yourself at a time when you have no experience with trust. But many have gone before you, lighting the way with a flame renewed by faith.

Lift your heads, close your eyes, and sing.

Personal Stories

JENNIE'S STORY

Both my parents were sex addicts. I learned a lot of what I know from an investigation because my parents are dead. My mother died when I was twenty-one, and my father three years ago. We grew up in a family that was on the surface strictly religious, teetotaling, and very handsome. We were an upper-middle-class family from the South.

My mother molested me as a child and, although I didn't realize it until just recently, my father participated as an observer. My mother got sick when I was pretty young and the disease she had progressed until she died. She stayed at home all those years until just the last two or three years before she died. Therapists I'm working with say, judging from her symptoms, that she may have been in the last stages of syphilis. I don't know whether that's true.

I do know that my mother was a sex addict before she and my daddy married. Daddy told me stories. The day before their wedding day, my mother went on a date with another guy. Daddy got real mad about it, but she just laughed at him and said, "I'll do what I want to do." He often said that she thoroughly enjoyed male attention, but that's all he would ever say. He was protective of her but as I grew up, he made veiled remarks about her behavior. He used to talk about what a beautiful woman she was and how popular she was and how it was a really big deal that she would even consider going out with him.

As far back as I can remember, sex has been used in some way to be abusive to me: it has always been this huge deal. Looking back, I know that other abuse had sexual connotations. I remember Mom's washing and scrubbing my body until I really thought my skin was going to fall off. She scrubbed me and scrubbed me and scrubbed me until I got those little bloody marks from her scratching too hard. I remember hating that, but it had no other significance for me. It wasn't until I was older that it stopped, and I still don't know what that meant.

Another thing she did was kind of strange. My hair was real long, and we had one of those curling irons that you literally stick in the fire. I had to look perfect all the time, and she would curl my hair and burn my head and just laugh about it. She also insisted that I sleep with her, so I did—I'm not sure how long. When I began recovery and started trying to remember my childhood, I couldn't figure out where I slept until I was five years old because there wasn't a bedroom in the house for me.

Finally, my sister got married and moved away, and I got my own room. Even then, my mother made me sleep with her until the second grade. When I slept with her, I had to be totally silent and endure whatever she chose to do to me, and that's when she molested me. What I figured out with my therapist is that it probably started when I was about four, and my best guess is that I was in the first or second grade when it stopped.

I sucked my thumb constantly, twenty-four hours a day, and I was real afraid of the dark. I used to have nightmares if I slept by myself. Once I got in trouble for something I had done at school and Mom came up there. She and my teacher made me stand up in front of the class and suck my thumb in front of everybody and they ridiculed me for doing it. They were trying to embarrass me to make me stop. I guess one reason that experience stands out is that she suddenly made me sleep in my own room, after all this time of sleeping with her. I didn't want to sleep alone because I was scared to death. I mean, I didn't want to sleep with her, but I didn't want to be by myself either. Somehow I connect that time with the thumb-sucking incident, as if she got mad at me somehow. In my memory it is all connected. So, it must have been between the ages of six and seven when she stopped molesting me.

In the beginning of her disease, when I was eight or ten years old, she could still drive and was reasonably functional. She had an affair with an elder of our church. She always met him at the cemetery after she picked me up from school. They met in the mausoleum, where they left me, and went off by themselves. After this had gone on for at least a year and a half, I finally got the courage to say something to my dad about it, and my dad tried to put a stop to it. After that, the guy just started coming to the house; it didn't stop Mom at all. That was the only affair that I personally know of. Based on her behavior though, before she was so sick she couldn't leave the house anymore, I suspect there were more affairs.

I grew up in the Church of Christ, so sex was very shameful; you would burn in hell for thinking about it. On the surface, my family was talking and acting that out, while underneath they were doing everything they said was horrible. By the time I was five years old, my mother was already calling me a slut, but I was a good child. I was always taught that sex is awful.

After my mother could no longer leave the house, the disease had progressed to the point that her behavior was really bizarre. She undressed in front of people, or she touched her body in sexual ways. There was always some kind of sexual suggestion in whatever bizarre stuff she was doing. My dad finally took her to the doctor. I think I was in school, but my memories are sketchy. I remember when my mom came back from the doctor. She was crying, and she called her sister on the phone. I'll never forget this picture. I'm in our hallway, sometime during the fifties, and she's sitting on the edge of her bed by the doorway, talking on the phone. I stood in the hallway watching her. She was crying, and she said, "God's punishing me for the things I've done."

For the next thirteen years, I watched my mother go totally insane, and I got a real clear message about what **God** does to people who aren't good enough. I didn't know what she had done wrong.

My father's reaction to all of that was total denial. None of that ever happened. He was always telling me that the things I had seen hadn't really occurred. Meanwhile, until I reached adolescence, my dad was like God to me. He was like my savior, compared to this crazy woman who beat me all the time and took me with her to see her boyfriend. Then during my adolescence, although I hadn't done anything wrong, my father started calling me a slut. I never understood why he got so angry if I talked to a boy. He would just get nuts. If I went out on a date, he stood in the driveway with a gun, totally bizarre.

Then he started calling my girlfriends sluts, and later I found out that he was having sex with them. He was—I don't know how to put it—he was being sexual with some and he had intercourse with some, but he made it seem that it was all their fault. They had seduced him somehow, and he was the innocent victim. I found out about it because some of my girlfriends told me. Dad told me too. He also told me openly about his sex life with my mother, who was by then a raving maniac with no sanity whatsoever. He said that he was still capable of sex with her and that she was insatiable. He could never measure up, sexually. I really acted out in my adolescence and became very promiscuous. Eventually I met my husband and married him.

I have what used to be a brother and a sister; my older brother had a sex-change operation. They are considerably older, and I don't really remember their being at home because my sister left when I was five and my brother when I was six. My mother fought a lot with both of them. Mom and my brother were all enmeshed and really close, despite the fights. She not only fought with my sister, who was about nineteen years old about then and working already, but she called her a slut, too. I remember Daddy's beating my sister once for wearing slacks because he thought she looked like a whore. My father beat the shit out of her. She doesn't remember that beating to this day.

After I went into recovery, I started wondering what happened to my mom when she was growing up. I've thought all along that it was strange I never questioned any of this. I did question my mother's bizarre behavior once I became an adolescent, but I just blamed it on her sickness.

I have done a lot of reading and research on my family origins during my therapy. I believe that my grandfather committed incest against my mother and all her sisters. One of my maternal aunts committed suicide at eighteen. The story is she went to Tennessee to stay for a few weeks with an older sister, and she wouldn't come back to live with her dad. He was a violent, angry man, and he insisted, so she shot herself. I have a sense, just from the little we've said about it, that he was incestuous.

During my adulthood, my father and I maintained a very close relationship. Our closeness had to do with his being alcoholic as well. I was very much the caretaker, sort of a wife to him. So he continued to tell me about his sex life until the very day he died. I didn't know there was anything abnormal about all that because I had grown up that way. My mother didn't talk much, but she demonstrated a lot. When I entered recovery and remembered my mom's acting out and her angry abusive talk to me, and my dad's sexual acts and confidences, I realized that my parents were sex addicts. That just blew me away. I hadn't known that there was anything out of the ordinary about their behavior.

So, here we are, a few years into recovery, my son and I. I'm working hard to understand how all of this is affecting me—my parenting and my relationships. I'm doing it for my sake and for my kids' sake. If we've learned anything, it's that we deserve a healthy, happy life, and we're willing to work for it!

THE STORY OF MIKE, JENNIE'S SON

I don't have any specific memories of ever being molested or anything like that, but some stuff is starting to surface now, having to do with my cousin and his sister. I just know that sex has always been a big deal in my life because I've been thumped on the head by my dad and mom too, who always told me when I was growing up not to do what they did. "Make sure you don't get anybody pregnant and don't get married before you're thirty-five." My dad was always suspicious and worried that my mom was cheating on him.

I just kind of caught wind of that. I remember everything he told me about sex—the subject was supposed to be very open. In the house, we talked freely about sex, but Mom hardly did at all. If I asked a question, she told me to talk to my dad. It made me real angry when the first date I ever had, my dad came out and said, "Here, use this for your first date," and sat this giant box of rubbers on the counter and said, "You're going to need this." I said, "No, I'm not," and he said, "Yeah, you are." He always said stuff like that.

I learned growing up with my parents that you don't show affection for anybody unless it's behind closed doors— nothing in public. I really didn't think I was anything like my dad until I got into a relationship with a girl, but it drives me up the walls to hold somebody's hand in public. I'm like a cat whose hair stands up on end. It drives my girlfriend crazy when we're walking through the mall, and she wants to hold my hand. I can do it for only about two minutes, and then I have to let go. I'm starting to work on that in therapy.

Another thing I did, every time a relationship with somebody started to get sexual, I quit. I learned how to use sex as a way to control people without ever having sex. I was kind of just the opposite of what guys are supposed to be. Instead of running around screwing everyone, I was a tease. I would get girls to the point where they wanted sex, and that was enough for me. I kept them around thinking and telling them, "Yeah, we'll do it tonight." With every girl I ever dated, I always left the door open so I could come back in whenever

I wanted to. It sounds like power and control, but it happened because I was scared or something. There was never any kind of panic or anything. Here were all these nice girls, and nothing was happening, so I went out with bad girls and still didn't do anything. I got real frustrated with that.

When my brother Todd was six and I was ten or eleven, we started "experimenting with girls," as my dad calls it. It was pretty weird because I was ready to do anything, or at least I thought I was. When I was ten, I played with the girls on the block until one in the morning, "experimenting." My little brother was going with me when he was about five or six. I kept getting in trouble for taking him with me but I still tried to sneak him out because he wanted to go. After awhile, my daddy said it was okay for my brother to go too. I thought it was weird that he was letting me stay out that late because he used to insist that I be home before the sun went down. Now it seemed to be okay for me to stay out late if there was a chance that Dad's son might "get some." At ten years old! I would come home and tell him stuff. I was all happy about my first real kiss for real and all that. When I told him about it, he said, "You just come in when you're ready and don't stay out too late."

The only thing my dad ever told me about when he discussed sex was "fucking." That's it. He never told me how to make love to somebody I cared about or anything like that. He told me, "This is what happens, you have an orgasm and the sperm swims to the egg." It was never anything romantic, and he never told me about how to be nice to someone I care about or anything like that. He only told me how to do the sex act.

I never saw anything nice or romantic go on between my parents either, not even anything sexual. The only thing I remember that had anything to do with sex was an old copy of *Playboy* in my dad's closet. When I showed it to my mom, she said, "That's a *Playboy*, and it's the only one your father has ever had, and he doesn't even like it." That's all I remember.

When all the kids who lived in our neighborhood started
screwing, I was real mixed up in that too. The girl down the
street was called the slut of the block, and I thought she was
pretty and went out with her for a couple of dates. I was still
ten or eleven. While I was going with her, I was still playing
with these other girls on the block.

There wasn't any actual sexual intercourse, but we played
"rape" and "dare" and "suck dick." I made up this game called
"rape." Even at ten years of age, I knew what sex was and I
knew how to do it and I was real locked into trying to get to
that point. (I never got there until I was about twenty.)
Anyway, rape was just like tag except that it was mostly to
catch a kiss or something.

I stayed overnight a couple of times with a kid who had
just moved in on the block. The regular way for his dad to
wake him up was to dive onto his waterbed and horse around
and wrestle awhile. They started wrestling one morning, and
his dad got Jimmy in a headlock. Jimmy hit him in the
stomach because it hurt, and his dad picked him up, jerked
his clothes off, dragged out the belt and hit him from his
head to his feet.

Jimmy was real sex-conscious. At one point he tried to get
my little brother, who was five or six, to have oral sex with
him. I knew the difference between right and wrong, but at
first I encouraged it, saying, "Yeah, that's it," but just before
he started to do it, I decided it was wrong and said not to do
it. So, I told him to quit, and he asked why. My little brother
just didn't know any better, I said, and it was wrong, and
Jimmy shouldn't do that. He went ahead and did it anyway,
and I jerked my brother off him and beat the shit out of
Jimmy, then beat myself up after that for letting it happen. I
felt bad for encouraging it. I've always known, as far back as I
can remember, what was wrong about sex and what was right
in my dad's eyes, and I knew this was wrong. And, for some
reason, I knew when I was going out with that one little girl
and still playing with the other three girls that it was okay
and I was allowed to do that.

Sex is my biggest handicap in relationships. Anytime I broke up with a girl, part of it was because of sexual stuff. She wanted to, but I couldn't. I could only fantasize about doing it.

I didn't have sex until last year. Then I "played Mr. Bunny Rabbit" for nine months. I'd have sex nonstop all day. I went crazy. It didn't bother me for about a month, but for about eight months, I felt like I was screwing my best friend or something. I really don't know how to describe it. It felt really bad having sex with this girl. It got to the point where I felt so bad about it, I couldn't stand to be around her, and I needed to get away from her. I did my best not to tell her I hated her, but I had to go somewhere and be by myself for a while. I always felt like I was cheating on myself or something. This last time I felt like I was cheating on myself or somebody else, which I don't understand. I think I have a lot to work through and understand about this whole area of my life.

I was always told that when it's right, I'll know, but it's never right. Now I've been in recovery from my alcoholism for about three years. I'm looking at myself as the child of a sex addict; I found out from my mom that Dad was a sex addict. If understanding myself as a child of a sex addict doesn't help me take care of these problems, I may change later if it turns out I'm a sex addict too.

MIKE'S MOM, JENNIE

I was thinking while Mike talked about the connection between his story and what I know was going on between me and his dad. We kept very quiet about sex in front of our kids. Mike's dad came from a very dysfunctional family with drug abuse and sexual activity. I'm not sure what the activity was, but I know something happened. When Mike's dad and I got married, I changed. I had been promiscuous as an adolescent, and when his dad and I got married, I was pregnant with Mike, and I turned 180 degrees and worked hard to be good.

Early in our marriage, when Mike was a baby, there was a lot of fighting and open discussion about divorce. During the first few years of our marriage, my husband constantly accused me of running around with other men and all kinds of other stuff. He was very violent and beat Mike a lot. One thing that neither Mike nor I were aware of until I began recovery was the triangle in our family relationships. Mike's father would insist on sex with me and, if for some reason or another I chose not to participate, he beat Mike. That took me awhile to figure out with my therapist. That was the punishment. If I didn't live up to his father's sexual needs in some way or another, Mike was beaten. I think that was unconscious on his dad's part, but that's what was happening.

At that time, I was trying to overcome my religious upbringing. I didn't take the kids to church because I didn't want to cram religion down their throats as my parents did, but even without that "churchiosity," a strict, rigid view of sex was there. Here was his father doing what Mike describes, and I was at the other extreme. What Mike said about the *Playboy* is true; I was a prude in a way. Also, I can remember when his dad had conversations with Mike about being responsible and giving him condoms. At that time, I was telling him that if he was with a girl he mustn't talk bad about her, but should treat her with respect. I was coming from my stuff and trying to tell him to be kind to women.

What was going on in our marriage was that there was absolutely no affection whatsoever. The only time my husband would touch me was when we had sex. Mike was totally accurate; there were no hints of affection publicly or in front of the kids. But, when that bedroom door closed, I was just raw meat for whatever my husband chose to do. What I've come to understand is that, to him, sex was love, and if he didn't get sex frequently, whenever he needed it, he wasn't loved and he would react in rages to that. So, I know my kids got a lot of confusing messages about sex. They had an angry, emotional, violent father who gave them a lot of the sexual, macho messages Mike talked about, and a totally shut down mother. I was trying really hard to look good and clean and be an honorable parent to the children, and the result of that was that I was totally shut down. My husband had a rule that my kids were not to discuss anything sexual with me.   I said, "Talk to your dad about sexual stuff." I honored that rule, obviously, and it was a real strict rule.

JOHN'S STORY

I was born in August 1950. The only thing anybody ever told me about my birth is my mother's repeated remark that I was the ugliest baby she ever saw. That bothered me a lot. I was the first of two children in my family. One other was stillborn and a fourth died after eleven hours.

I don't really remember when I first noticed that my mother and my father drank a lot. While my mom was pregnant with me, my dad was hit on the head with a piece of iron and was in a coma for twenty days, and the doctors didn't expect him to live. I've often wondered if that changed him.

When I was growing up, fighting, drinking, and raising hell was a part of life. I didn't like giving pain. Most of the time, I let other kids beat me up rather than fight. When I was ten years old, Max was my best friend. We often stayed overnight at one another's house. Once even Max beat me up. A lot of the other kids started calling me chicken shit because I didn't like to fight. I did wind up fighting a lot, but I always hated it.

I guess I probably started drinking when I was twelve, and that made me more susceptible to trouble. One kid at school jumped on me in math class, and I saw red. When I came back out of it, I had busted every tooth in his mouth (he had to get false teeth), and I was sent to the principal and had to see his mother and dad. He'd been after me all year and I had just had it. I remember starting to do weird things after that.

When I was ten, I was promoted from the fourth to the fifth grade a few months before school got out, and I never knew why, so I was a year younger than the other kids in high school. I remember fighting another boy and whipping him the first day of school in junior high, but I really don't remember details, it's as if I blacked out. We later became really good friends. His family went to church a lot, and they were weird people.

My sister was beautiful and still is a very pretty girl. I was always taught to be the protector, older brother, you know. When I was about nine years old, I began noticing that my mother and dad would go off drinking; they were always gone. They would say, "Don't say shit to nobody." My mother was always complaining about us kids, saying that we always bothered her. I just tried to take good care of the house and my sister.

The first time my dad beat my mother up we were living with my grandmother. My mother wouldn't get out of bed so Dad was yelling at her to get up and fix us kids breakfast, and he beat her up. I remember wondering why he did that. My grandmother just sat there and kept her mouth shut. My grandmother was like that her whole life, and I never respected her.

There was lots of sexual stuff going on too. One day while we were living with my grandmother, the neighbor lady came over in just her housecoat. I wasn't very big, but I remember my dad's foot was up this woman's housecoat, between her legs.

I've seen my mom naked all my life. She used to walk around the house naked a lot. She started talking to me as I got older about her and Dad's sex. All I remember is that she didn't seem very happy about it. I remember hearing them one night in bed (they were making love with the door closed) and I heard her ask him to kiss her breast. She used me for a sounding board. I was always the one she came to when she was angry or hurt, and she often cried on my shoulder. For a long time, I hated my dad because of this. I thought, "Why didn't my dad just treat her like she wanted to be treated?" The bad part was that my mom would come up to me and shake her tits in my face and say stuff like, "How about these titties! Aren't these great titties?" I didn't know what to do or say. What kind of mother would do that to her boy?

There came a period where my mom would get all dolled up to go out all the time, and my dad was basically never home. He was always asleep when he was home, or else he was out working or drinking. I took care of my sister and raised her. I was the one who cooked and kept house. My sister was nineteen or twenty years old before she ever learned how to cook or clean because I did it all. My mother was a good cook when she wasn't drunk. When she came home and we watched TV, it was her TV and when we listened to the stereo, it was her stereo. If we hid in our bedrooms, she'd say, "What in the hell are you doing in the bedroom?" We weren't allowed to swear.

My dad beat my mom up on a regular basis, and my sister and I sat up all night and worried about her. Finally, one day I ran my dad out of the house with a shotgun because he'd dragged her around by her hair. Then I had to take her to the hospital.

When I was about fifteen, I began to understand why Dad beat her. She was a party girl. He'd go to work, she'd go party. My dad and mother were both extremely jealous of each other. Whenever she took off with her girlfriends to get drunk, they put us in the car, and whenever they passed a carload of guys, they make us kids duck down, so the guys couldn't see us. Once a guy beat me up, and my mother sat there laughing.

When I was fourteen my dad went away and worked somewhere to make extra money. Right after he left, my mother left for three or four days with three guys. Life went on; I took care of my sister. Then they came back and one of the guys took me and my sister out to the barn. I realized later that the other two were in the house screwing my mother.

I was an underachiever. I didn't even try. I guess I was four years old when my mother taught me how to read, but that's all I really wanted to do. I read books in school instead of paying attention in class. I could read and listen at the same time, so I could answer the teacher's questions and still be reading. The history teacher asked me once how I could do that, and I said I didn't know. But I always thought I was stupid. I guess I just really didn't want to try. I worked in a supermarket and a five-and-dime store and doing other odd jobs. I always had money and my sister knew she could get money out of me if she wanted a new dress or something else.

My mother passed out a lot. She had three stages: she had her social drinking; the second stage was super bitch; and her third stage was passing out. As super bitch, she hit us, and then she passed out.

I'd bring my friends over to drink and she'd come home and be really pissed off. One night I called her a whore, and she called one of my friends an ugly bastard. Some mother!

When I was fourteen my mother passed out often. Sometimes people found her unconscious on the front lawn and helped me carry her into the house.

At about this time, my sister quit talking to me. She was extremely angry toward men, but I think she's grown out of it now. When she first started dating, I met several guys that she went with. They were really nice, treated her really decent, and she walked out on them, used them, and took money from them. She's a real user for money. She's owed me so much money in the past and still owes it. She doesn't ever pay it back.

My sister doesn't call my mother "Mom"; she just calls her by her name. It's as if they were two peas in a pod when they get together. They can't stand the thought of each other. But if you look at my mother and my sister, it's as if you're looking at twins, with only the years separating them. Their actions and speech are the same.

Growing up, my sister never would say anything about what went on. Whereas I was a worrier, she withdrew. She didn't seem to feel anything. It didn't seem to bother her when mom came home all beaten up and all. She withdrew and didn't say anything. It was as if she was never really a part of it. While I was passive and allowed myself to be beaten, she was the violent one; to this day, a lot of people are scared of her. She would attack in a heartbeat and wouldn't give a damn who you were or what you wanted, man or woman. While we were growing up I kept wondering, where was the brother-sister relationship, because she had the characteristics of the big brother image, like fighting. I tried to be her big brother and take care of her.

I remember a horrible thing between me and my sister. It used to be such a damn thing that I never did figure it out. I wouldn't come near her friends or touch them. I used to come in when my sister and her friends were practicing all the new dances, you know the twist and all the other dances kids were doing. Anyway, they'd dance in the living room and I'd be sitting there reading. They danced over and shook their butts in my face and tried to entice me, laughing and giggling, and my sister would walk into the room and immediately yell, "Rape!"

I never did understand why, but I felt betrayed and angry. I can't really express all the feelings I had about it. My parents immediately jumped on me about it, and I hadn't touched anyone. The more my sister did that, the more enticing her girlfriends became. After a while, when I saw her girlfriends come in, I left the house to get away from them. There were several other times when she got me beaten up for stuff I hadn't done.

When I was four or five I was sexually abused by three Mexican men. They all went into a building with me. All I really remember about it is the fact that they went to the pen for it. I can't remember what happened, whether there was any shame involved in it or anything else. It just popped up in my memory while a lady was talking at a workshop I went to.

I was sixteen when I had my first girlfriend. My daddy gave me a sex talk that was very stupid. The first time I masturbated, he walked into the room, and I was so ashamed. In his big sex talk, he had told me to masturbate, but when he saw me doing it, he said I was disgusting. At sixteen I couldn't stand living at home anymore. I didn't get along with my parents, and my sister and I had grown so far apart. She didn't like any of my friends and said her friends were better. She only wanted my money; otherwise, she left me alone.

My dad never shared anything with me. The only person who told me anything about his childhood was my grand-mother. I tried to talk to my dad, but he always told me to keep my mouth shut. The whole time I was a kid, my dad came to only one ball game I played. I saw him, and he turned around and walked off.

When I was fifteen or sixteen, my parents separated for a while. Mom kept my sister, and I stayed with Dad. One Christmas Eve, Dad came home drunk, asking "How was she?" I asked "How's who?" He said, "Your mother, how was she in bed? You laid with the bitch, how was she?" Then I stormed out of the house. I used to be able to rationalize, but this time I lost control.

Several times I tried to run away, but I always went back. I started hanging around with a tough crowd. I didn't fit because I didn't like to fight, and it was kind of weird that they accepted me when nobody else would. I did get into some fights, but I really don't remember them.

I still saw my mother. She was very critical. People didn't get very close to her. I'd walk in and she'd be drunk and start in: "You bastard, you son of a bitch!" Christmases were always especially hard. Then I joined the Marines. I had to find out whether I was a man. Vietnam was going on, and I went over there. It was a kind of living hell. When I came back here, I was different.

The first time I had sex was overseas when I was nineteen years old. I used to worry that I might be queer. When I came back over here, I met my first wife. She was a super socialite, and I was on leave, and she was in college. She was the first woman I ever loved. She invited me to an informal party, meaning to me jeans and a T-shirt. The other men were in short-sleeved shirts with ties and I wanted my ass out of there. The guests were a lot of people she knew, and there were champagne and cocktails, and I just sat on a chair by myself.

I went back into the Marine Corps, and she went back to her friends. We never had sex. Then I got into some drugs and drank a lot.

When I left the service, I went home and after six months, I married my second wife. Then I found out she was a nymphomaniac. We had sex seven or eight times a day while I was home on leave, and she always wanted more. I really don't know why I married her because I was not in love with her. Just one of those things. We were married approximately eight months. She was crazy!

Dad's sexual escapades were a little more covert than my mother's. When I was sixteen, I had a car, an old Biscayne, I think. I had a blanket across the horrible back seat. When I came home from work one night, Mom was gone. Dad came over and borrowed my car because his was low on gas. The next morning I went out there, started to get in the car to leave, and noticed that the blanket was all messed up. I started to straighten it out and found a pair of panties lying there. I mean, I wasn't stupid, so I stuck them under my shirt and walked through to the bathroom and handed him the panties. He said, "Did your mama see this, you son of a bitch? I'll kill you if you tell her." I just turned around and walked out because by that time, I was used to the bullshit.

Later on in life, I can see it was kind of a shame between me and my sister that Dad had a girlfriend. He had her for years and still has her today. He bought her a car and makes no bones about it. Mama knows about her. The woman's name is Ronnie, and I went to dinner with her. Ronnie is a neat lady, ugly as hell, but she does what Dad wants. Dad became impotent, and I could understand that. My mother bitches continuously, and an article I read once claimed that bitching is one way women castrate men. From the time Mom wakes up until she goes to sleep at night, she's constantly bitching. It drives me screaming mad and I can't handle it, so I can see where it would . . . I know it would make me impotent. I couldn't rest with a woman who constantly bitched at me. So, as far as I know, they haven't had sex in years.

Dad's had several girlfriends. My parents broke up again when I was in boot camp, and the only letter I ever got from my dad was when he told me my mother had tried to commit suicide. I tried to get out of boot camp to go home, but they wouldn't let me. While my dad and mother were separated, he had another woman and her kids living in the house with me and my sister. They went places like Carlsbad Caverns. My dad never did such stuff with us, and we were kind of jealous.

While I was in the service, Mom and Dad got back together after about a six-month separation, and he started going with Ronnie. I don't understand Dad's and Mom's relationship. For a long time, they slept in separate bedrooms. Ronnie has never been in their house as far as I know.

AUTHOR'S NOTE:

I had special dealings with John, whose story you just read. I first met him in a meeting, where he stood towering over everyone, with his arms folded over his chest and a look on his face that was half glaring and half inviting.

He and I attended a workshop, and I ended the week thinking that I had met few people in my life willing to work so hard for the life they yearned for. I also observed a powerful group of people in the local Twelve Step community who embraced this man and each other in everyone's desire to heal and change. I'll never forget him, as his tears began to come, genuinely bewildered, saying, "I was a good boy. I didn't want to hurt anyone. Why did it have to be like that?"

Toward the end of the workshop this man brought a poem he'd written the night before. He'd spent his day sharing his story with us and it affected him powerfully, and kept him awake that night to write this poem for us.

JOHN'S POEM

My little child is still there, I know
For he never had a chance to grow.
His face is balled up in pain
For he is covered in shame;
Shame and guilt for things
He didn't do or deserve
But how is a little child to know?

His eyes are red and swollen
From tears that still flow.
He wants so much to stop crying,
To laugh and play as other children do.
But he doesn't know how, you see.

He wants so much to love and be loved;
To come out from the dark room where he hides,
A lonely place where no one else can go.
No one can hurt this child anymore.
But he is so alone and afraid,
For every time he stepped out of this room
Instead of love, he got pain.
Sometimes I see him, just a quick glimpse.
A shy little child who runs away quick.
Sometimes I feel his tears and fears
Sometimes, late at night, I think I can feel
Him crying
And I feel so sad.
I want to touch him.
And to hold him
To wipe his tears away
And to tell him that I love him
And that I won't let anyone hurt him anymore.

But when I reach for him, he runs away.
You see, he's really afraid of the man he hides in,
The man he has become.
This man is full of so much rage
That he scares the little boy.
This man knows the child's pain
But doesn't let it show.

He never lets anyone know that he cares or feels,
For to do so invites pain,
To be hurt once again.
So, the man wears different masks.
Sometimes a clown, always laughing loud.
Sometimes his mask is that of anger, to
    keep people away.

He wears many masks each day,
Each designed to keep people away.
He's a lot like the little child,
For he's always ready to run away.
He would like to reach out
And once again take a chance,
But, like the child, he's afraid of pain.

I pray to God that he hold this child close
And give him a chance.
For I love this little boy and I'm trying
Hard to let him know.
For I know now that, if I can love him,
Maybe we can both grow,
And the pain and hurt may go.

If this were only so,
The masks might fall away
And then I wonder what I
And my little child might see
And be.

So, little one deep inside me,
Lie down to rest.
Don't be afraid.
Try not to cry.
You're not alone anymore,
I know you're there
And I love you
And I promise I'll protect you
And give you a chance to grow.

I know the pain and shame,
And I also know you're strong,
For there's strength in pain.
Hold tight to what little I can offer
And together our love will grow.

Good night, my little child.
Sleep tight.
I love you.

About the Authors

Rick Lair Robinson is currently director of the Gateways Treatment Program in Roseburg, Oregon, where his wife, Barbara, is presently involved in outreach activities.

Rick began his fifteen-year career as a chemical dependency counselor and family therapist. This background has helped him develop and direct programs for adults, families, and adolescents, for both inpatient and outpatient programs.

Rick brings the gifts of humor and understanding to his writing, training, and therapy.

Barbara Lair Robinson began her education and training in 1980 at St. Mary's Junior College in Minneapolis, Minnesota. She remembers the director of her training program, Jeff Lupient, saying, "We're going to do something different for the chemical dependency field. It's called Family Systems Approach." She is forever grateful for this foundation.

After several years as a family counselor, Barbara has enjoyed developing Employee and Student Assistance Programs, teaching and training counselors, writing and lecturing, and working with families.

THE TWELVE STEPS OF ALCOHOLICS ANONYMOUS

1. We admitted we were powerless over alcohol — that our lives had become unmanageable.
2. Came to believe that a Power greater than ourselves could restore us to sanity.
3. Made a decision to turn our will and our lives over to the care of God, as we understood Him.
4. Made a searching and fearless moral inventory of ourselves.
5. Admitted to God, to ourselves, and to another human being the exact nature of our wrongs.
6. Were entirely ready to have God remove all these defects of character.
7. Humbly asked Him to remove our shortcomings.
8. Made a list of all persons we had harmed, and became willing to make amends to them all.
9. Made direct amends to such people wherever possible, except when to do so would injure them or others.
10. Continued to take personal inventory and when we were wrong, promptly admitted it.
11. Sought through prayer and meditation to improve our conscious contact with God, as we understood Him, praying only for knowledge of His will for us and the power to carry that out.
12. Having had a spiritual awakening as the result of these steps, we tried to carry this message to alcoholics, and to practice these principles in all our affairs.

THE TWELVE STEPS
Adapted for Adult Children of Sex Addicts

1. We admitted we were powerless over the sexual addiction troubling our families, and that our lives had become unmanageable.
2. Came to believe that a Power greater than ourselves could restore us to sanity.
3. Made a decision to turn our will and our lives over to the care of God, as we understood God.
4. Made a searching and fearless moral inventory of ourselves.
5. Admitted to God, to ourselves, and to another human being the exact nature of our wrongs.
6. Were entirely ready to have God remove all these defects of character.
7. Humbly asked God to remove our shortcomings.
8. Made a list of all persons we had harmed, and became willing to make amends to them all.
9. Made direct amends to such people wherever possible, except when to do so would injure them or others.
10. Continued to take personal inventory and when we were wrong, promptly admitted it.
11. Sought through prayer and meditation to improve our conscious contact with God, as we understood God, praying only for knowledge of God's will for us and the power to carry that out.
12. Having had a spiritual awakening as the result of these steps, we tried to carry this message to other adult children of sex addicts, and to practice these principles in all our affairs.

REFERENCES

Bass, Ellen and Laura Davis. *Courage to Heal.* New York: Harper and Row, 1988.

Beavers, Robert L. *Psychotherapy and Growth: A Family Systems Perspective.* New York: Brunner-Mazel, 1966.

Carnes, Patrick J. *Out of the Shadows: Understanding Sexual Addiction.* Minneapolis: CompCare Publishers, 1983.

Carnes, Patrick J. *Contrary to Love.* Minneapolis: CompCare Publishers, 1989.

Cermak, Timmon L. *Diagnosing and Treating Co-Dependence.* Minneapolis: Johnson Institute Books, 1986.

Cermak, Timmon L. *A Time to Heal*, New York: Avon Books, 1989.

Clancy, Tom. *The Cardinal of the Kremlin.* New York: Berkley Books, 1989.

E., Stephanie. *Shame Faced.* Center City, Minn.: Hazelden, 1986.

Fossum, Merle A., and Marilyn J. Mason. *Facing Shame: Families in Recovery.* New York: W.W. Norton, 1986.

Lechler, Walter, and Jacqueline C. Lair. *I Exist, I Need, I'm Entitled.* New York: Doubleday, 1980.

Lerner, Harriet. *The Dance of Anger.* New York: Harper and Row, 1985.

Schwartz, Sc.D., Mark, and William H. Masters, M.D. Selected papers.

	The Illusion of Normality	Mistaking Excitement for Intimacy	Control	Interactions Are Sexualized
Addict				
Co–addict				
Family as an Environment				
What the Children Learn and Take into Adulthood				

RESOURCES

Sexaholics Anonymous (SA)
P.O. Box 300
Simi Valley, CA 93062
818/704-9854

S-Anon
P.O. Box 5117
Sherman Oaks, CA 91413
818/990-6910

Sex Addicts Anonymous (SAA)
P.O. Box 3038
Minneapolis, MN 55403
612/871-1520

Adult Children of Sexually Dysfunctional Families (ACSDF)
P.O. Box 8084, Lake Street Station
110 E. Thirty-First St.
Minneapolis, MN 55408

> Write the above address for ACSDF newcomer packets, information on starting a group in any state, long-distance sponsorship. Please include self-addressed stamped envelope.

Twin Cities Codependents of Sex Addicts (COSA)
P.O. Box 14537
Minneapolis, MN 55414
612/537-6904

> For national information on COSA, write the above address. Please include self-addressed stamped envelope.

Incest Survivors Anonymous (ISA)
P.O. Box 5613
Long Beach, CA 90805
213/422-1632

Golden Valley Health Center
Sexual Dependency Unit
4101 Golden Valley Rd.
Golden Valley, MN 55422
612/588-2771
Toll free: 800/321-2066